To Dana
Love like you've never been hurt
and
"Keep on Dancing"
Best Wishes
Bob Smith
10/27/10

you gotta
DANCE
like no one's watching

LESTER H. SMITH

with Trish Morille

bright sky press
HOUSTON, TEXAS

2365 Rice Boulevard, Suite 202,
Houston, Texas 77005

ISBN: 978-0-9819904-1-5

10 9 8 7 6 5 4 3 2 1

Library of Congress Cataloging-in-Publication Data on file with publisher.

Creative Direction by Ellen Cregan
Design by Wyn Bomar; Illustrations by Mike Guillory
Printed in China through Asia Pacific Offset

you gotta
DANCE
like no one's watching

A two-time cancer survivor and two-time national ballroom dance champion takes life for a spin

LESTER H. SMITH

with Trish Morille

Like Father, Like Son

by Trish Morille

In January 2009, I was working with Lester on collecting his stories for this book when he blurted out something that dumbfounded both of us. He said, **"You know, Trish, I don't really think I have accomplished that much in my life."**

"I mean, I've been pretty successful in the oil business, but what else have I done that really means anything?"

Having worked with him for the last seven years on numerous large grants and donations, I didn't know what to say.

"Lester, what do you mean? **You're the most generous man I know.** I was there from the beginning, when you launched the *Honor Your Father Campaign for Prostate Cancer Research*, to the establishment of the Lester and Sue Smith Breast Center. Not to mention the **hundreds of other donations and gifts** you made along the way."

As I ticked off the names of contributions made to the medical community, the arts and education, as well as humanitarian endeavors, it became vividly clear to me that those gifts, while incredibly meaningful, **did not represent the mark of successful philanthropy Lester envisioned or sought.**

We both left the meeting that afternoon in deep thought, reflecting on what "accomplishment" really meant.

In preparation for our next meeting, I decided to make a list of all the contributions Lester and Sue had made. Even I was astounded when I saw it all on paper for the first time. I went over the list with Melissa Reta, Lester's office manager.

Melissa is one of the brightest, most upbeat and funniest women I know. And she doesn't miss a trick. A good asset for those who work with such a sharp guy.

"Babycakes, you're missing a few," she said.

And with that, she pulled out a file.

"This is Lester's Puppy File." She handed it over to me.

I spent the next two hours looking at notes, letters, cards, copies of emails and photographs. My favorite was a crayon picture of a pink angel with wings, drawn in a child's hand.

Each card, note or drawing was yet another look into the generous spirit of a man whose philanthropy knew no bounds.

There were handwritten letters in pencil from a Midland Boy Scout troop that otherwise couldn't afford to go to camp. Notes from eight college students whom Lester supported with full four-year scholarships. Cancer patients who were grateful for both kind words and entrée to top-ranked medical professionals. A thankful young attorney whom Lester met at Starbucks was on his way to a Smith-organized job interview.

And the angel drawing?

Melissa explained, "Oh, that was for the iPods."

"iPods?" I asked.

A new maintenance man was working in the office, and Lester struck up a conversation with him. The man had evacuated from New Orleans after Hurricane Katrina, with barely the clothes on his back. In typical Lester style, he asked about the man's family and learned that he had two daughters who loved music. Lester sent the man home with two iPods for his little girls, already downloaded with great tunes. **And in return, they gifted him with that precious drawing.**

I looked at my long list of Smith Foundation–supported organizations: Baylor College of Medicine where the Lester and Sue Smith Breast Center and the Lester and Sue Smith Urology Clinic were named in their honor; the Smith Gem Vault at the Houston Museum of Natural Science; the Smith Distinguished Lecture Series at Holocaust Museum Houston. Scores of endowed chairs to further cancer research for both children and adults at Texas Children's Hospital, Baylor College of Medicine, MD Anderson Cancer Center and educational initiatives at Ben Taub Hospital.

A routine exam at Memorial Hermann after Lester's heart attack in 1999 resulted in a large grant for the University of Texas Health Science Center. The Lester Smith Cardiovascular Training Center was established, an unprecedented training ground for physicians to learn about PET imaging and preventing and reversing atherosclerosis.

Hundreds of other gifts went to support an A-to-Z list of non-profit organizations in Houston and around the United States, from 20,000 Christmas bikes for underprivileged kids, to gifts of support to victims of domestic violence. There didn't seem to be a non-profit that had not benefitted from the Smiths' largess.

There were personal gifts, as well. Money to pay for funerals, and to help out a former Wharton neighbor who had fallen on hard times. There were checks to help a single mother with childcare so she could go to college, and even funds to pay for dental and medical expenses for total strangers.

The stories Lester has collected here are a glimpse into his heart, and I am grateful that he allowed me to help share them. But **as I write this, I know with complete certainty that Lester may never fully understand the depth of his generosity. It truly knows no bounds.** His struggle was never with giving the money away; that was the easy part. His challenge was simply how to do more.

His struggle was never with giving the money away; that was the easy part. His challenge was simply **how to do more.**

Getting the First Word In

by Sue Smith

As Lester's wife, it's unusual to get the first word in; but then, he always gets the last! Seriously, Lester is one of those "larger than life" people who go after life with zest. And although he's had more than his share of illnesses, he has never let them get him down for long. He never whines and says 'Why me?' but moves forward with enthusiasm however he can. To him, life is *always* worth living, and living with a smile. I feel very blessed to share a life with such a dynamic and loving man.

To give you an inkling of what he's like, here is a little poem I wrote for his birthday about fifteen years ago before we were married. It'll give you a glimpse of who he was then and still is! I am honored to say a little something about my husband before he takes the floor.

LESTER

It's nice you're 52
You're better now at everything you do
Trials and errors are in the past
Hopefully maturity and passion will last
You've driven fast cars
Hit the bars
Been so wild
Acted like a child
Been a shit
Thrown a fit
Run the show
Wouldn't let go
Played your quirks
Acted like a jerk
Crossed the line
Had to bide your time
Been so low
And let it go
Been so high
Thought you could fly
Gambled your money
Called me Honey
Been so sweet
So happy we could meet
Held my hand
Been my man.

The Last Last Word

by Lester Smith

I was asked to submit an editorial piece for *The Houston Chronicle* for **National Philanthropy Day,** November 13, 2008. I scratched my bald head for many long hours trying to figure out what that big word meant. As I write now, our nation is still facing some pretty tough economic times, and I think my thoughts are as relevant now as they were then:

Thursday, November 13, several hundred Houstonians will converge in a hotel ballroom to celebrate National Philanthropy Day. I remember the first time someone **referred to me as a philanthropist.** *It wasn't that long ago, and since I can't spell my way out of a wet paper sack, I had to look it up. I found "philanderer" first and thought I had been insulted. Thank goodness for my wife, Sue, who handed over the reading glasses and eased my mind a bit. She knew what the words meant at first glance. Both of them, and without glasses.*

Philanthropy is **a fancy way of saying "generosity."** *And Houstonians are a generous bunch indeed.* **We raise millions of dollars each year** *to support many non-profit organizations—from critical research in the Texas Medical Center to arts organizations here and even across the pond.*

But how do you **inspire people to give** *during such tough economic times?*

How can we give when our glasses are not only half empty, but there seems to be mere drops left?

As a second-generation Texas oilman, I have seen both the boom and bust of the oil business. Growing up in Wharton, **my father was my first example of philanthropy,** *although he wouldn't have known what the word meant either. He just knew it was the right thing to do. There was always room for one more at the dinner table, and sometimes two or three. There was always a family to support, a child to clothe, a job to be given.*

My first real math lesson *came when I was around eight years old. There was a tamale vendor, Felipe, who supplemented his weekly job by selling tamales on Saturdays. Tamales were six for fifteen cents or twenty-five cents for a dozen. My dad would hand me a quarter and tell me to go and get six tamales and "let Felipe keep the extra ten cents." It didn't take me too long to figure out that I could get a dozen tamales with a quarter. When I questioned my dad's counting ability, he simply said, "That's all you need. Felipe needs the change more than we do."*

16

My brothers, Stephen and Alec, and me during our college years. Well, at least we looked smart!

When my dad died, his office manager showed us a file in his office. In my dad's bold, deliberate handwriting, were **page after page of loans he had made with no intent to recover them.** *We saw the names of migrant workers who came to pick cotton in the fields of Wharton. We saw notes of new business ventures, people suffering the ravages of disease, jobs lost and spouses who had died.*

My brothers and I each inherited $500, but more importantly, we **became heirs to a philosophy of life and philanthropic spirit** *that molds each of us to this day. That humble sum was a life lesson in giving that far surpassed its face value.*

We also saw our father in a light that continues to shine on in our own work and lives. For it was his example that has inspired us to generosity of both treasure and heart. And that was probably the best lesson I have ever learned: that there are many ways to give, but **giving first comes from the heart.**

Sometimes it means writing a check, sometimes it means giving time, sometimes it means denying ourselves just a bit so that others can benefit. It also means being sensitive to a challenged donor base during difficult times.

The non-profit community will do well to foster new forms of giving and inspire a challenged constituency to think outside the donor box. As parents and grandparents, we must **encourage our families to give,** *but more importantly, model it to them. And we as a community must "hunker down," as the good judge says, during these difficult times and remember that giving takes on many spirited forms.*

This was one of the proudest moments of our lives when Colin Powell presented us with the National Association for Fundraising Professionals (AFP) Excellence in Fundraising Award in 2006 for our work on behalf of the Honor Your Father Campaign for Prostate Cancer Research.

So, consider what you feel passionate about. Is it fund-raising? There will always be dollars yet to be raised for vital causes. What about volunteering? There are thousands of opportunities for you starting today. **Want to inspire others?** *Go out and teach. Good at reading, writing and arithmetic? Mentor a child. Not only will our community be enriched, your life will be too. And in the end, you will be a living, faithful example of what true service means in this community we are all blessed to call home.*

After all, **the antonym of philanderer is "faithful."** *I know, I looked it up.*

20

Lester H. Smith
Op-Ed, Houston Chronicle, November 13, 2008
Association for Fundraising Professionals,
National Philanthropy Day Celebration,
"Change the World with a Giving Heart"

And in the end, you will be a living, faithful example of what true service means **in this community** we are all blessed **to call home.**

This book is dedicated to my precious wife and dance partner, Sue.
You have taught me to embrace the dance of life at every turn.
And to my family, friends and all those challenged by cancer —
may you be inspired to dance like no one's watching.

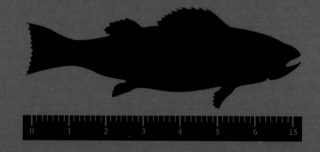

[1]

fish stories

I lay curled up in a ball, **sobbing like a baby,** thinking I was about to die from cancer. My thoughts led me to all the things I would never get to do. I'd never get to grow old with my little sweetie girl: my life partner, my best friend, **my drop-dead gorgeous wife, Sue.** I'd never get to see my children again or watch my beautiful grandchildren grow up. I'd never win another ballroom dance competition, climb Mt. Everest, chair a record-breaking gala or hit that fabled oil well in West Texas.

I would never become the richest person in the world or president of the United States or King of the Universe. I would no longer get to serve on the board of directors of our homeowners' association or the board at the country club or be president of the synagogue. (Of course, getting off all those boards was just about the only positive thing my imminent demise offered.)

My life was over, and what did it all mean anyway?

That's when it hit me. Literally.

Sue slapped my face and said, "Like hell you're going to die! We have some living to do! Now snap out of it! And I mean it!" And I collapsed into her loving arms. But I won't go into that right now.

Okay, I have been known for my fish stories. She didn't really slap me—that hard. It wasn't like she said, "Hey, buddy, I'm going to kick your butt!" It was more like, "Get a grip, you blithering idiot!" **Or something loving like that.**

All my life I have been known for my gift of grand expression—or maybe it's the gift of exaggeration. Whatever you call it, I totally **blame my dad.** He would take me fishing, and boy, could he make up some good fish stories. There was the ubiquitous "one that got away" story; there was the fifteen-inch, one-and-a-half-pound trout that grew to at least twenty-eight inches. Thinking back, I'm sure it was a bit bigger than that, weighing in at four pounds, no, make that five. Well, that's what I think it weighed, but our scale was always a little off—on the light side. Once I told that fish story over and over, it was gospel

26

That's my father, Maynard Smith, in his early twenties.

I signed up for a life of family, friends, dancing, great experiences and memories, more stuff than I could count and more riches than imaginable, and great jokes and storytelling.

truth. My sweet wife, Sue, always tells people not to believe my **"fish stories,"** the size of the new well, how many hours a day I work out, and on and on. My God, I can never get her to play along! "Hey, baby, how about cutting me some slack here? After all, I might kick off any minute! Give a guy a break, and let him go out with a couple of good fish stories tucked under his belt!" She just doesn't understand how Texas oil guys have this gift of exaggerated gab, the wonderful ability—skill, even—to improve the actual facts.

Alright, then. I'm busted. Sue didn't actually slap me. She grabbed my shoulders, gave me a slight shake and said, "Lester, I'd know if you were going to die, and you're not. **So snap out of it!"**

And here I am, sharing my stories with you, and I've already blown my cover. Didn't even make it to the second chapter. It's the story of my life. But believe me, keep reading. I'll sell you on something before we're done here, and you won't even see it coming. I love storytelling, and there's nothing better to my ears than hearing, "Wow, Lester! Tell me more, and where do I sign?!"

I guess after all these years, Sue and I know what we signed up for. I just didn't see the big "C" looming in our future. No, what I originally signed up for was a life of family, friends, dancing, great experiences and memories, more stuff than I could count, more riches than imaginable, great jokes and storytelling and always starting sentences with "I." As in, **"It's all about me,"** or "I think" or my personal favorite, "Enough about me. What do *you* think about me?"

So I wasn't about to let some little old "C" word get in the way of "me." I know that sounds self-serving, but when you are looking at **"sayonara, baby,"** believe me, that's what you're thinking about. What *you* are going to miss out on.

If I kicked the bucket, I'd be missing out on way too much. And I thought, "I'll be damned if I let cancer get me now. It is not time to go. I have a lot of 'Lester' living to do."

I had battled bladder cancer for nearly two decades, but it was my diagnosis of aggressive prostate cancer in 2001 that nearly pulled my plug and had me planning my own funeral. Thanks to God, that event will be planned at another date and time. In a seventeen-year period I was in the operating room under general anesthesia more than forty times. Now I'll tell you, that wasn't any fun. And you know what? **I got it,** I understand, I've been there, and believe me I know how very precious life is. I'll never be ready to go. You don't get it until you get it, and I got it. I still have way too much living to do. One year at a time, one month at a time, one week at a time, one day at a time and, what it really boils down to, *one moment at a time.* **That's how I live now, and it's just glorious.**

My doctors at Baylor College of Medicine in Houston were key to my beating the disease. I had a first-rate team of outstanding physicians who I truly believe helped **save my life.** And today I live my life like there literally is no tomorrow. I can honestly say, if the good Lord takes me today, here's what I know: I've been deeply in love with my

30

survivor:

A person who continues to function or prosper in spite of opposition, hardship or setbacks

My mother and father in the Emerald Room at the Shamrock Hotel, 1953. They loved watching entertainers like the Andrew Sisters and Milton Berle at what was called "Houston's Riviera."

wife. I've been both a total disaster at fatherhood, and at times that surprised even me, I've been really loving and engaged with my kids. This is due in large part to the fact that they have a pretty great mother. Their mom—my college sweetheart, Barbara—and I have been apart for more than twenty years. She was a wonderful wife, partner and mother, and she will always have a special place in my heart. Last Christmas, Sue invited Barbara and her husband, Bill, to our home in Colorado, and she spends every Passover in our home, too. We are on one another's "joke of the day" email list, and we end every telephone conversation and personal meeting with a heartfelt "I love you." And we do.

But, back to me. I've achieved some notoriety as a **champion ballroom dancer,** and I have a few trophies and titles on my wall to remind me that all those dance lessons I grudgingly took as a kid paid off.

I have eaten way too many hotdogs on the streets of New York, waiting for someone to give a young man a break, and I've gotten a few breaks; I've been not only rich, but filthy rich. Okay, that's another fish story but I am still rich enough to have my own hotdog stand. But only one. I might have been filthy rich, but—stupid me— I gave a lot of my dough to private wealth managers in 2006–2007 and didn't read the contracts carefully. I should have looked on page 138, where they were also described as *private wealth destroyers*. Where are those jokers now? **Where is my dough?!** I like to kid those guys, no make it that I would like to break their kneecaps. My stack of chips is certainly smaller. But I'm alive, living in the moment and there's always another day. It's only money, you didn't eat me and I'm healthy as a horse—my Russian dance instructor used to say, "Strong like Russian bull." Are there bulls in Russia? I don't know, but I do know that I'm very much alive, and **I just love my life.**

And now, it's time to give what dough I have left away. No, not *all* the dough, but lots of it. Mostly, I want to give the lessons I've learned during my marathon battle with cancer. I hope that in some small way, you will benefit from my experiences, too.

So that's what all these meanderings here are all about—giving it away. Giving away the pearls of wisdom I gathered when I heard "you are going to die" way too many times. Actually no one—no doctor, no nurse, no friend or family member—ever said those exact words. But, my God, that is sure what I heard and what I thought and believed with all of my heart and soul. That is the worst kind of fish story.

Here are my thoughts and **the life lessons** I have learned at the black door called cancer. Cancer is ready to rob anyone in its path of the precious gift of life, ready to steal hopes, dreams and end the dance forever. But with Sue there to slap some sense into me, I have kept dancing.

While it all sounds so poetic, which is not my way at all, what I have really learned—maybe the hard way—is to let go, to make each and every day count and to **dance like no one's watching.**

My Russian dance instructor, Vika, with me in 2003 when I won the Over 50 Men's International Standard Competition, a title I held for three years. The International Standard is a series of five dances—the waltz, viennese waltz, tango, foxtrot and quick-step.

Dancing the cha-cha with Sue at the 2003 United States
National Championship in Minneapolis-St. Paul.

I hope that each of you **reading my stories** will love more deeply, laugh a lot longer and find the perfect music for your **own dance of life.**

2

god help me

I am a lousy Jew. No, I'd better rephrase that: I am lousy at *being* Jewish. As I have progressed in my "spiritual walk," I realize that I have never been a very observant Jew. I might have been a better Buddhist. According to my Buddhist friend Tran, the **purpose of life is to end suffering.** Tran says we continually suffer from our desire for things that don't provide true and lasting happiness.

I am all about true and lasting happiness; and of course, ending suffering is pretty high on my list, too. It's the part about "things" that I struggle with. Because, like many people I know, **I love my stuff.** The trappings of all my hard work—and yes, my good fortune—are all around me. Is that so bad? I think it depends on how you use your good fortune.

Maybe I should have been a Catholic. Actually, outside the Jesus as Messiah issue, we are pretty well aligned. All those great rituals, the challah and wine, you get the picture. But the purgatory thing—I just don't get it. I've asked some of my Catholic friends to explain to me that place where our souls are "purged" of sin so we can enter the pearly gates. Me? I'd like a one-way, **first-class ticket to heaven,** please. And charge it.

A while back, I was flipping through the 80,000 channels offered on my cable service, when I came upon a handsome young man with an enviable full head of hair. I wasn't sure if he was an evangelist or a salesman. Maybe a little of both. Please understand me, being a convincing marketer of your beliefs is not a bad thing. If you truly believe that you have the best [fill in the blank: *widget*, *religion*, *service* or *product*], you got it—you da man! This guy almost had me converted. It all sounded great! He said there is only one God—that makes it easy even for me to understand. Wealth is okay—what matters is what you do with it. **We are all sinners—yep, that's me.** We can all be forgiven—and we can all get to heaven. Sign me up.

40

We decided to "ink it up" for our Biker, Babes & Blues party. Check out the fake tattoos!

I believe in God, admit that I am not perfect (and never will be), but like I always say, "I am a work in progress." Aren't we all?

This brings me back to Judaism. You don't find much about heaven in the practice of Judaism; our focus is on the here and now, and frankly, I like that. **I believe in God,** and admit that I am not perfect (and never will be). Like I always say, "I'm a work in progress." Aren't we all?

I don't keep kosher, and I rarely attend services. I had a Bar Mitzvah, but I think they just passed me in Hebrew school to get rid of me. Maybe that's why I'm still such a kid. I'm still **trying to grow up** at age sixty-eight.

I was taken to Hebrew school and services in Wharton, and I spent more time trying to figure out how *not* to go than to be present and accounted for. Unless I am talking, my attention span lies somewhere between thirty and thirty-one seconds. It must have been easier for everyone to simply let me do my own thing.

Maybe that's why I'm not so good at religion. I always hear more about what *not* to do, than what *to* do. My good friend Stan Doctor explained it best when he told me about a thousand times, "Lester, you're what we call a 'closet Jew.'" My answer back was always the same, "But Stanley, I went to Hebrew school and I had my Bar Mitzvah, so **I am Jewish.** Plus, no one ever put me in a closet—well, not for that long!"

Many times when I've told people that I'm Jewish and grew up in a small farming community in South Texas that had eighty Jewish families, they would say, "But your name is Smith. That's not a Jewish name." And I would always reply, "Yes, I know Smith is not a Jewish name, but we changed it when I was young." Now I had them going.

The shrimp was on the hook, and the hook was in the water. One hundred percent of the time, they would ask, "What was your name before it was changed to Smith?" And without batting an eye, I would answer flatly, "Jones." We would all hold our sides in laughter. I still use that joke to this day, and the response is still the same.

Russell Gordy, my business partner of twenty years in the oil and gas business, grew up on Houston's north side, the son of a Houston police officer. Russell's goal in life was to make $18,000 per year and not take any crap off of anybody. To say he has done slightly better is an understatement. He is as smart as a whip and as tight as a . . . well, **the bark on a tree,** and he doesn't have an anti-Semitic bone in his body. One day we were negotiating a deal and I was really trading tough, asking for the world and hoping we would get 10 percent of what I was asking for. I was on fire.

At a break, Russell took me aside: "Lester, I've never seen you negotiate so skillfully. If I didn't know better, I'd think you were Jewish."

I stared at him blankly. Of course I was a skilled negotiator.

"I *am* Jewish," I replied.

"Right," he answered. "Your name is Smith, and you're from Wharton, Texas and I've been your partner for over 10 years. **I'd know if you were Jewish.** There aren't any Jews named Smith in Wharton. And I haven't seen you heading off to synagogue much."

He was right, of course, I didn't go to synagogue much. How could I be Jewish?

laughter:

An expression or appearance of merriment or amusement

It's not a sin to make a lot of money, if you act with integrity and strength of character. What counts is what you do **with the money.**

I pointed out my heritage. I explained how my grandparents had come over from Russia in the early 1900s, settled in Wharton with eighty other families from Eastern Europe and established one of the earliest Jewish communities in that area.

Yes, even if I didn't practice it, **I was born and raised Jewish.**

He said, "Well I'll be damned. No wonder we've made so many good deals."

"Russell," I told him, "my Jewishness has nothing to do with my deal-making. I'm just a really good deal-maker.

I've never checked Russell's heritage, but he could be a Jew, too. He has absolutely put me to shame when it comes to being a tough trader. He just doesn't let people take advantage of him; it's his way or the highway, and he gets his way nearly all the time. And truth be told, he is a wonderful person and the best business partner I have ever had—**his handshake is his bond.** Maybe he's a closet Jew, too. "Gordy" sounds a lot more Jewish than Smith.

Our conversation made me think about something important: with a name like Smith, or Jones, I wasn't subjected to the same anti-Semitic remarks that I so many of my friends and family endured. As a boy, my family wasn't allowed to join the Wharton Country Club, but since so many of "us" were instrumental in bringing commerce to the town, that didn't last long. None of us ever joined. We had the Jewish Community Center and that's where we all hung out.

I don't know what a Jew acts like, or a Christian or Hindu for that matter. I only know that we are supposed to try and **live the best life we can,** and to show compassion and respect for other people. It's not a sin to make a lot of money or to negotiate hard for it if you act with **integrity and strength of character.** And when you make it ethically, what happens next is natural—you learn to let it go. You learn the importance of sharing what you have with others. It's what I am doing right now that counts.

I don't wear my religion on my sleeve, or my chest, or my car's bumper. I believe that the true mark of a person isn't his religious branding or her church affiliation; it's what's in that person's heart. I can't stand religion being shoved at me, or anyone for that matter, and I hate that people argue over which God is best. There is only one God. Period. And what I've seen is that He is good and constant and ever-present, even when I am missing in action.

Intolerance of others' beliefs has led to horrible crimes and wars and unrest, and it deeply saddens me. Can't we simply respect that we have differences and focus on the good in one another? There are people to this day who spend way too much time and energy thinking about how we are different; I say there is **too much that binds us.**

And mostly what binds us is our common experiences and what really sticks us together like glue are our **common challenges.** I started going to AA decades ago. I've had a few slips, but I've been sober since my last big cancer surgery in 2001.

Life is HARD.
But life is GOOD, too, especially when you know you may not have much of it left.

When I first went to meetings, all the God stuff made me absolutely crazy. God knows me, yes. God loves me, yes. And I believe God brought us here for a reason, and yes, He saves us at certain times in our lives. But God gave us a brain and a heart and the rest is because of hard work, day after day. Life is hard. But I have discovered life is good, too, especially when you know you may not have much of it left.

When I was diagnosed with cancer, I did begin to see my life in a new way. Okay, you could say, **"Lester finally saw the light,"** but it wasn't like some kind of religious conversion. It was that time had different meaning for me. All the little crappy things that used to make me crazy don't quite make me as crazy today. I learned to act as if what I was doing would make a difference. And the first step in making a difference was letting go of the stuff that was holding me back from being **truly happy and at peace.** I learned to let go of lots of stuff. And when I found out how much fun it was to let go of the green stuff, there was no turning back.

Letting go of the money is fun—you should try it! Start with something small. An extra buck or two for a tip, or offer to pick up someone's tab at the coffee shop. Tell your dry cleaners what a great job they did on your shirts and give them a big tip, or surprise your spouse with something they've been wanting and tuck a little love note into the package.

You know the old saying, **"you can't take it with you."** I know it's true. You can't take the money with you. But what you can take with you today is the feeling

50

Victoria Belova from St. Petersburg, Russia, and I dancing the tango.

Here we are dancing like no one's watching at the Texas Challenge.
Actually, there were hundreds of people watching our every move!

that you are helping make a huge difference in the life of someone by giving whatever you can—**time, talent or treasure.** The returns are great—better than you can ever imagine. Because it's real, baby. Whatever religion you are, or aren't, your reward will be here—and in heaven—and wherever your heart is. **Trust me on this one.** I swear to God it's true.

3

my seventh birthday

I have been told that **I have a memory like an elephant,** especially when it comes to numbers, dates and the smell of crude oil. I suppose that may be true; after all, there are pigs that can sniff out small bits of black fungus buried underground, and when they're brought up, they cost about the same price as a barrel of oil. Sure seems a lot less complicated than what I do for a living. **Now there's a thought . . .**

YOU GOTTA DANCE LIKE NO ONE'S WATCHING

It's true that a **scent can often transport us** to days gone by and trigger a wellspring of emotion long buried. Like the classic conditioning experiment made famous by Pavlov, I simply drool over the smell of crude. Okay, there's another comparison: Lester is a pig *and* a dog. I've been called worse, believe me.

Music has the same power over me. And together? It's magical. The scent of Shalimar and the song **"Earth Angel"** are blasts from my past that bring me right back to the Wharton Country Club.

I was thirteen years old, and her name was Sharon, and she wore a purple velvet dress. She was tall, with long, dark hair and the bluest eyes I had ever seen. I don't recall much else about that night, except that the dance floor was huge and I had fallen madly in love. Ah, puberty! Falling in love was a daily occurrence. But Sharon was different. She was The One—the girl I wanted to spend the rest of my life with. Foolish boy! I could spell L-O-V-E, **but could I spell raging hormones?**

That sweet-scented memory prompted me to attend my 35th high school class reunion and drag the real One, my knock-out wife, Sue, along for the hour-long ride to Wharton. Undoubtedly Sue had heard Sharon's name a million times.

Since those gloriously hot and heavy days in Wharton, things had changed a bit for me, but the **dance floor still loomed prominently.** Sue and I had taken quite a fancy to dancing and had become competitive ballroom dancers. The night of the reunion, she wore some glittery earrings and I wore some, too: a gold loop in my left ear

My older brother, Stephen, and I in 1948 at Raven Ranch Boys Camp.

Now, this is what a dancer's hot bod looks like. Check out her awesome abs!

with a diamond stud nestled alongside it. More is better, I say. But, hey, we were Latin dancers and that is how Latin dancers dressed: solid black from head to toe and lots of bling. I guess I missed the note on the invitation that stated, "No tattoos, nose rings or double piercings." Good thing no one could see my belly button.

We stuck out like a **diamond in a goat's nose.** That massive dance floor I remembered at the country club was about the size of a postage stamp. But my memory of that enchanted evening was still sharp. I took Sue to the exact spot where I had danced and fallen madly in love with Sharon. It was the northwest quadrant of the postage stamp.

"This is the spot, Sue. This is where I met Sharon," I said, wistfully. "She was so tall and beautiful in her purple velvet dress, and she smelled like heaven. She really was an Earth Angel."

A tap on my shoulder brought me out of the heavenly clouds and back to earth. Standing before me was a short, older woman with wiry gray hair and chocolate brown eyes twinkling behind her wire-rimmed glasses. Beaming at me, her hand covered her name tag and she giggled, asking, **"Guess who?"**

I absolutely hate guessing games; my memory for names and faces is about as short as . . . well, you go and figure it out. It was short.

She removed her hand, and there in all her glory, stood my tall blue-eyed angel, Sharon. I felt like a fool, again. Sue looked at me with that wonderful smile, you know the one that says, **"You silly jackass."** I was glad she still loved me, even if I told fish stories to myself.

So my memory occasionally fails me when it comes to women, but my memory for oil wells is like a steel trap. One whiff of crude oil brings back the memory of every well that I have ever drilled. And I'm talking about from age seven to the present day. I love crude oil nearly as much as I love women; in fact, both my testosterone and my crude-oil hormones rage out of control to this day. How about that, **sixty years of raging crude-oil hormones?** And the smell of crude beats the hell out of Shalimar any day.

That's the way it was in Wharton. It could indeed be crude—in more ways than one. Humor was as dry as one of our fields. We used to say that if you listened long enough, you'd hear those fields crying out in the summer, "Water! We need water!" We were a cotton community, and we lived and died by the rain. No rain meant a bad business year for the merchants in Wharton. But we were also a community bent on finding out what lay beneath those cotton fields. And that is why I decided to **make my fortune** in the oil business.

One of my earliest memories took place on one of those typical hot, dry days. It was August 16, 1949, my seventh birthday. That day I decided to become an oilman **just like my dad.**

My father and I were out on some rural property, about ten miles southeast of Wharton at the Boling Salt Dome. The baked clay-like soil left little to the imagination,

memory:

The length of time over which recollection extends; the act or fact of retaining and recalling impressions, facts, etc.

My cousin Judy, brother Stephen and I in 1945 in the family swimming pool.

except to an oilman and a boy with a shoebox full of rocks—and a mind some might say, full of the same thing.

To my dad, the fields of Wharton were lush with the promise of oil; to me, those fields revealed **a certain kind of magic,** in the form of the shiny bits of quartz, calcite and fossils I collected and stashed in that old shoebox.

I kept that box of rocks underneath my bed for years. I would take them out every once in a while to study them and marvel at how Mother Nature made rocks glitter so much. Later, at about age thirteen, I took the rocks out of the box, put them away in the garage, and filled that box with *Playboy* magazines. I took those magazines out of that box every day and marveled at how **Mother Nature made those girls glitter** so much. From that time on, my collection of rocks stayed stagnant while my collection of magazines grew exponentially.

An oilman is really nothing more than a treasure hunter. There's not much difference between a guy panning for gold and a guy like me who likes to see what lies—or flows, as the case may be—underground. My dad and uncle, and many of our neighbors, were all cut out of that same cloth, too. We're all fascinated by what lies below the surface of the earth. And bringing it up to the surface? It is like Christmas; and that memorable day, it was the **perfect birthday celebration.**

I awoke very early that day, ready to go at the crack of dawn.

"Is it time to go, Daddy?" I whispered. I already knew the answer. Dad was still

63

asleep. I glanced at the clock. 5:00 A.M.

"Hmmm? What? Time to go? Not yet, son," my dad answered. "We'll go later today; I'll let you know when." He rolled over and went back to sleep.

An hour or so later, as I waited impatiently at the breakfast table, the same conversation ensued.

"Dad, when are we leaving for the oil well?"

"Lester, I told you that we'd be leaving later today, and it's still not late enough. Now go on and play and I will call you when we are ready to go."

"But why does it have to be later?" I'm not good at waiting, never was.

He gave me the finger. The index one that said "don't harass me any longer, or else." I knew that finger well enough by age seven.

It was pretty late in the day when my dad finally called me in and said it was time to go. I don't think he had even finished the sentence before I was running for the garage.

The sun was already pretty low in the sky, but I didn't care. We were heading for the rig. For a young boy intent on following in his father's greasy footsteps, it was **heaven on earth.** Where else could you get completely dirty, stay up all night and listen to the rig workers tell tall tales of their escapades across the border?

My dad used to say that oil wells were like babies: they were always born at night. And that night was no different. We hopped in the pickup truck, an old red Ford with

I love this photo from 1949 when I was just seven years old, taken with my mentor and wildcatter father, Maynard Smith.

a missing taillight, and headed out of town, just as the sun was starting to sink in a cloudless sky. A few dirt roads later, we were there.

On the way, my dad gave me the **"oil rig facts of life"** story. They were dangerous, they were dirty and noisy and I had to stay clear of the workers. I promised him a hundred times over that I wouldn't get in the way, and of course, I would be extra careful.

The first thing you notice about an oil rig is its smell. My dad jumped out of the truck's cab and the first thing he did was stop and take a deep breath. He breathed it all in—the smell of the mud, the grease and the iron. Those are smells that will stay with me forever. **I love that smell.** One whiff and I am brought back to that day. It is completely invigorating, very nearly an aphrodisiac.

There was another smell indigenous to this area—sulfur. This particular well was smack dab in the middle of a sulfur patch. The Boling Salt Dome is a 5,000-acre underground salt dome and rock structure with the claim to fame of having produced more sulfur than any other mine in the world. The Texas Gulf Sulfur Company began mining it in 1928 and eventually established its own town, Newgulf. Now a ghost town, in its heyday, it boasted 350 homes, **a movie house, and even a golf course.** Over 8,000 wells have been drilled to mine sulfur there, and hundreds more for oil and gas. Huge blocks of sulfur dotted the dry landscape, as large as a football field, creating an almost surreal picture. The smell was very real, however: the smell of rotten eggs.

father:

Paternal protector or provider; a man who exercises paternal care over other persons; a male parent

Even the water had a sulfur taste to it.

The second thing you notice is the noise. Sulfur starts out below the earth's surface as a solid. Using the Frasch method of extraction, steam was pumped into the ground to melt it, and then the liquid sulfur was pumped out to the surface and cooled to a solid again. Drilling for oil was also a noisy process. Back then, there were two large steam boilers that ran off of diesel; these ran the drilling rig. Between the knocks, bangs and vibrations, you could hardly hear all the **great cuss words** the rig workers were saying. I learned to read lips at an early age. While I never finished my Spanish language courses, I am proud to be fluent in Oil Field Trash Talk.

It was always **hot and muggy,** especially in August, but the hottest place by far was the Dog House, a windowless shack or cabin decorated with girly posters and ripe with the earthy smell of grease and sweat. I'm pretty sure those girly posters fostered my growing collection of *Playboy* magazines later in life. But I won't digress.

I loved hanging out with the rig workers. They gave me Hershey bars and saved their favorite rocks to add to my growing collection. I was fascinated by how many of them had lost a finger or two, a testament to the dangers of their work—and I envied their lifestyle. They taught me the **finer points of tobacco chewing;** it was a really nasty habit, but I thought it would make me a big, tough oilman. Add a pint of Kentucky bourbon in your back hip pocket and then you were *the man*. No wonder those roughnecks had some missing fingertips. Handling heavy steel drill pipe, chewing

68

tobacco and swigging bourbon all at the same time made an already dangerous job an accident waiting to happen.

After a couple hours of hanging out at the drilling site, we were getting ready to leave for dinner when we smelled the faint odor of fresh crude oil. **Daddy and I ran down to the mud pits** and we could see the slight shimmer and gleam of crude oil floating on top of the drilling mud that was contained in the pit. He ran his hand lightly over the top of the mud and there it was: bubbling oil, black gold, Texas tea. He rubbed his oily hand on my face and smeared it with oil.

"We're close, Lester. We're close," he said, his voice barely containing his palpable excitement.

"Daddy, what do you mean? Close to what?"

"Close to the oil, my young oilman, close to the oil, boy."

Oh my goodness how excited I was!

"What are we going to do now, Daddy, what are we going to do?"

"Well, son, we're going to leave and go into town and have a chicken fried steak for good luck. You hungry, boy?"

Hungry for a **chicken fried steak smothered in gravy** with mashed potatoes and biscuits? Of course I was hungry.

It was the start of another drilling ritual. During the course of the next eleven years, we always left the rig and went into town for our lucky chicken fried steak with mashed potatoes and biscuits. Did it help? I'm not so sure; he sure drilled lots of dry holes. But there was always the backup bourbon.

If it was a good well, the pint of bourbon came out of nowhere and we all took a swig. And if it was a really, *really* great well, we took a couple swigs. It was an oil field rite of passage back in the old days. A dry hole meant even more whiskey; you know, **to kill the pain.** It is amazing how fast you can fill up on a dry hole. More amazing still at how many bottles seemed to come from hiding places all over the rig—or back pockets.

On a dry hole, that entire pint of whiskey disappeared, and of course there was always an extra bottle or two in the truck for those really costly dry holes. The combination of those dry holes and whiskey sure did cause a lot of oil field trash talk. Oh my, I didn't know there was such a multitude of **curse word combinations.** But what do you expect? It was a very high-risk business: one day you were rich and the next day you were flat broke.

I just hate dry holes. Show me someone who likes them and I will show you an oilman who has sold more than 100 percent in the well. Those dishonest fellows plugged many a fine well and were off to find a new set of investors to cheat out of their money. They didn't last long in our business. Why didn't those fellows figure out that you can skin a sheep only once, but you can shear it twice a year? But there were, and will always be, unscrupulous promoters around; I say avoid them like the plague.

As we drove back up to the field **fat and happy,** we were met with a glorious

"Well, son, we are going to leave and go into town and have a chicken fried steak **for good luck. You hungry, boy?"**

sight; the rig worker we had left in charge was covered in oil. He was holding a black, oily rag that used to be my dad's white handkerchief. It was a pretty good sign. We had hit the pay zone, we had found the oil. It was my Daddy's first well, my first well, and right then and there I set my first goal in life: "I want to be an oilman when I grow up, just like Daddy."

"Lester, come here," my dad yelled over the noise. It was already twilight but rig side lights kept everything in midday cast. He took my hand, put it in the mud pit again and rubbed his two hands together. His hands were dripping with oil; the pit was covered by a thick layer of black ooze. We found the oil zone, and it was big. Oil all over the place. Oh, how wonderful the smell, and even better, **the look on Daddy's face.**

"It's oily," I said.

A huge smile spread over his face.

"That's it, son. Now, smell it."

It was unlike anything I had ever smelled before, not unpleasant, just different and new. The smile on my dad's face reassured me that whatever I smelled, it meant oil.

"Is it oil?" I asked.

"It's Texas gold," he answered with a broad smile.

I was down there all night with my Daddy as we logged the well. Every report came back the same as the first. I still have the report in my desk drawer. The ubiquitous bottle of whiskey was produced and a celebratory toast rang out. Everyone, from my

72

dad to the rig workers, was rubbing that oily mud on their faces. It was like some kind of Native American ritual: their white teeth glowed; their voices rang with giddy joy and excitement. Whiskey and cash bonuses for everyone. **What a joyous sight.** I remember like it was yesterday.

"What are we going to name the well?" someone asked.

My dad answered.

"Well, it's my son's birthday and his first well. I guess we'll have to call it 'Lester's Well.'"

And while the paperwork named the well as C.M. Allen Well #1, it was always affectionately known as "Lester's Well."

I fell asleep in the cab of the truck, both exhilarated and exhausted. It would be the first of many such nights in the cab of the truck.

"You know what I want to be when I grow up?" I asked my dad as we drove the ten miles back to Wharton early the next morning. "I'm going to be an oilman like you and drill oil wells," I said.

My dad winked at me.

"Lester, there's nothing like it," he said. "It's not easy, and it takes a lot of patience and hard work. But when your well comes in, it's just about the most exciting thing ever."

Dad was right. He was thirty five years old when he made his first oil well; I was thirty three. And many wells later, dry holes and gushers, the **excitement of that**

73

seventh birthday lingers like the smell of crude.

I can't begin to count the number of dry holes that I have drilled over the years. Certainly there were times I was flat broke, ready to throw in the oily towel. But what truly kept me going was the goal I had set on my seventh birthday. It was, and it remains, a promise to myself. Sometimes I didn't exactly know how I was going to reach that goal, but I kept working and followed my nose. My instincts, even back when I was a little boy, were strong: they led me to the career and to the woman that were both just right for me.

Make a promise to yourself and set a goal. It doesn't make any difference what you do or what the goal is, just set a goal. Then work hard, and then work harder. When you get busted flat on your butt, get up and dust yourself off and try again, and again, and again. Nothing pays off like shear persistence. Goals and hard work always lead to success. Don't ever give up, just keep trying and think about what it is going to feel like when you achieve that goal. Because you will. Your well will can come in, too. And who knows? It could be a gusher. Mine was!

74

goal setting:

*Establishing specific, measurable
and time-targeted objectives;
a disposition that causes an
intrinsic drive to be delivered in a
professional manner*

Don't ever give up, just keep trying and think about what it is going to feel like when you achieve that goal. **Because you will.** Your well will come in too. **And who knows?** It could be a gusher. Mine was!

In 2003, we came back to defend our title and brought home the gold once again, winning the 2003 United States Senior Latin Championship.

[4]

give it the old harvard try

After graduating from Wharton High School, I followed my brother's lead and headed north to the University of Oklahoma. To say that I was a student **not quite living up to my potential** is a gross understatement. I was bent on two things, making money and not making the grade. I worked hard—but not at math or science. God knows I failed at English and writing papers. **I worked hard at having fun.** But I did learn a few things.

YOU GOTTA DANCE LIKE NO ONE'S WATCHING

I learned that I only had three speeds—stop, slow or real fast and stupid. I tended to stick in the latter gear. I also learned that most of my sentences started with "I." I was thinking of naming this book *It Is All About Me, So What Did You Expect* or better yet, *Me, Me, Me*, but *You Gotta Dance Like No One's Watching* won out—darn that publisher. So, back to the "I's." I learned that I was really good at doing numbers in my head—still am. I learned how to cut classes pretty well. I learned how to double my money betting on football games. Nah, not really. I learned much later that **if you really want to double your money there is only one foolproof way:** Fold it over and stick it in your pocket. But mostly, I learned that going to college was more about pleasing my parents than pleasing me. So, lacking just a few hours to graduate, I headed back to Houston, ready to make my mark in the business world.

I got **my first big job** in 1971, as a salesman for Lehman Brothers when it was just a partnership and not a public company. Along with Goldman Sachs and a few others, they were the kings of Wall Street. I was based in the Houston office, concentrating on oil and gas securities and making a pretty decent living at it. Those were good times. It's hard to imagine that just three decades later, the Lehman Brothers I remember so well would file for bankruptcy—the largest bankruptcy in U.S. history.

But back then, I was learning about the oil and gas business, not at the ground level in the fields of Wharton, **but at the high-rise level,** calling on clients in Texas, Oklahoma and Louisiana. Talk about some characters!

I learned that I only had three speeds—**stop, slow or** real fast and stupid. Guess which one applied to me?

intuition:

*Direct perception of truth, fact, etc.,
independent of a reasoning process;
a keen and quick insight*

I was calling on a guy in Midland once, delivering a sure-fire way to make a good return on an investment in an oil deal. "And here's how you are going to get your money back," I said.

This old gray-haired man with horn-rim glasses leaned over his desk, stared me down and said, **"Sonny boy, I already have my money.** If I don't give it to you, I won't have to worry about getting it back." He was just one of a blur of tough customers I pitched over the years, but meetings like that were great learning experiences that kept me on my toes.

After that slowdown, I practiced with some of my Lehman Brothers buddies. I got so good at pitching deals, the managing partner of the Houston office, along with some other Lehman Brothers partners from New York, bought my first oil deal. We ended up making four or five good wells! That always provides a little job security.

After several years, I decided it was high time to strike out on my own. Call it intuition or luck, whatever it was, **the timing seemed perfect.** Three months before the oil embargo, I struck out on my own. Oil was $5 per barrel and went to $39 by the early 1980s. As luck would have it, and yes, a little bit of planning, too, prices just felt too high, money was way too easy to raise and there was more money chasing deals than there were deals to be made. Well, let's really get straight about one thing here: I would much rather be lucky than smart, and big time lucky I was. So I cashed out in 1982. I completely sold all my oil and gas properties at the top of the market—

something I heard my dad say at the dinner table time and time again: **buy low, sell high.**

I heard that a time or two. But what my dad really tried to pound into my head was this: "Go east young man."

When I was eighteen years old, hanging out in the oil fields of Wharton with my dad, he always said this: "Lester, if you want to really make it big in the oil business, you have to leave Texas and go to New York. **You need East Coast investors.**"

But I wasn't ready to work that hard. I had been in the oil business from 1973 to 1981, a grand total of eight years; all I knew was easy money and great times. I was thirty nine years old, I had a pretty nice nest egg and I didn't have to beat the streets any longer. Who needed East Coast investors? I was headed for easy street, not Wall Street. I shut down my office, gave everyone a nice little package and announced that I was retiring.

For eight days, I had a really good time. It seems all a blur now, but it was a heck of a lot of fun while it lasted!

The rest was pure hell. It was the most miserable, depressing time of my life. I felt that I had abandoned my child, my baby—the oil business. What was I thinking? I couldn't retire. I didn't play golf or Parcheesi, and I looked horrible in a leisure suit. So I did what I do best—went back to work. I took an office in downtown Houston. It was considered a Class "C" building, but it was more like an "F." The elevator was so

84

truth:

Conformity with fact or reality; accuracy; actuality or actual existence

slow, I used to tell people that my office was fifteen minutes from downtown Houston. Eventually, the building got a facelift, but as my daddy used to say, **"You put lipstick on a pig, it's still a pig."**

In business, the old saying is timing is everything. It's true of life, too. By the mid-eighties, oil prices dropped to about $9 a barrel. In desperation, I turned to Jack Carter, my former boss at Lehman Brothers, for advice. **"What should I do, Jack?"**

Jack must have been channeling my late father. He said, "Go to New York and start calling on investors there." Reagan was in office, and despite the gloom in Houston, it was business as usual in the Big Apple. In fact, those East Coast guys were making money hand over fist. They were on fire. Jack agreed to make one phone call on my behalf, to George Baker.

I had never heard of him, but I trusted Jack.

I dug around and found out that George Baker was the fourth such named Baker from a long line of financiers. George Fisher Baker established the First National Bank of New York in the early 1860s. In 1934, *Time* magazine called him the richest and most powerful commercial banker in the U.S. When Harvard wanted to establish a business school, they sent a contingent of trustees to visit this Baker. "How much do you need?" Baker asked. **"Six million, sir,"** they answered. The story goes that without blinking an eye, old Baker said, "Put me down for it." The Harvard Graduate School of Business is named for him.

Talk about intimidation.

But I sucked it up and headed to New York and met George Baker, IV. We became **immediate friends and business partners.** He told me, "Lester, I'm going to introduce you to every 'white shoe' investor in the city." Hell, I didn't even know what he meant. I learned pretty quickly that it means large, powerful, financially-stable financial firms and high-net-worth individuals.

I started making monthly trips to New York and spent a lot of time with George Baker as he took me by the hand and introduced me to some of the most powerful financiers in our country. Here I was, a college dropout from Wharton, Texas, meeting men who dictated financial policy and headed up huge endowments. During that time, I learned a lot about how—and how *not*—to do business in the circle of "white shoes."

Once I was in a meeting at a private club in Manhattan. I started taking out some papers from my coat pocket when a client said, **"Put those away, Lester.** This is not the place to use pens and papers."

It was a delicate balancing act, but I was a quick study. And I was totally bent on being successful. I just had to learn to stand a lot and eat a lot of hot dogs.

You see, these were busy, powerful men. I had to catch them when I could. If that meant staking out their offices, I was willing to do that. I can't tell you how many times I stood around eating hot dogs on the streets of New York, waiting for someone to give me five minutes of their time. It was a deeply humbling experience, but one that **molded me well.**

Yep! That is exactly where I used to eat my lunch when I was in New York—and to boot, all by myself.

One of the toughest and most colorful characters I met in New York was Robert Stone. **His office was in Rockefeller Center,** probably because he got a good deal on the rent; the building bears his wife's family name.

I hung out trying to have a meeting with Stone, week after week, month after month, for one full year. Finally, after way too many hot dogs, probably a few extra pounds and a hell of a lot of patience, Stone agreed to a meeting. **I had two minutes.** When I entered his office, he never even offered me a chair. Not to mention a cup of coffee. Nope. He just looked at me from across his huge desk and listened—for two minutes. He wasn't buying that day. Or the next, or the next. Over the next year or so, he would give me two minutes to make my pitch and then his secretary would show me the door. She was nice, but she didn't let me sit down either. But I never gave up.

"Mr. Stone, can you give a young man a chance?"

Finally, after a year of these two-minute encounters, Stone offered me a chair. **I was speechless.**

He agreed to a small working interest in a gas well I was drilling in West Texas. Thank the good Lord, it was a success. Thereafter, he always offered me a chair and even an occasional cup of coffee when he was feeling generous. Sometimes I even had four or five minutes. I learned to talk fast.

I put Robert Stone in a few more West Texas deals, **some good, some not so good.** But once he made eight or nine wildcat wells in a row, things were bright again.

persistence:

Continued existence or occurrence; the continuance of an effect after its cause has been removed

One day, we were actually sitting in his office, drinking coffee, and going over the results of the wells. He turned to me and said, "Lester, do you know who I am?"

Was this a trick question? Sure, I knew who he was . . . or so I thought.

"I'm on the governing board of Harvard" he said. "I serve as the managing director of the Harvard Management Company, the university's investment arm."

My heart was racing. My knees were weak. If I were standing, I would have collapsed. Thank goodness he had finally let me have a chair before he told me this.

"I want you to go up to Boston and talk to Harvard about getting in the oil business with you."

Naively I asked, "How much money do they have Mr. Stone?"

"Three point eight billion," he answered.

"But Mr. Stone, I can't invest all that money!"

Stone started laughing so hard, he was nearly rolling on the floor.

"No, Lester, you won't get all that money, only a part of it."

He went on to explain, "Lester, when you do business with Harvard, it will be the equivalent of having the Good Housekeeping Seal of Approval on your forehead."

He was right.

I walked into the hallway, pushed the elevator button and broke down and cried. I had always been outside looking in; now I was on the **inside looking out.** I finally had my big East Coast investor.

Hell, all those times I was in New York no one would even go to lunch with me. I had stood on the corner of Wall Street eating hot dogs. No one would ever see me, and no one would give me a chance to **prove myself.** Until now.

The following week I went to Harvard. I met one of the head money managers of the Harvard Endowment. His name was Scott Sperling, and I thought he was a cocky little 28-year-old kid. We actually became good friends and remain so to this day. How was I to know that Scott had a master's degree in mathematics, was a Harvard MBA and knew every trading and negotiating trick in the business? Sure, Scott is a wonderful guy, but on the first deal with Harvard he sewed my pockets up tight, and Harvard ended up making all the money.

92

I wasn't about to become discouraged.

Instead, in 1986, I established my own company, Smith Offshore Exploration Company, and did my first deal with Harvard to drill for natural gas offshore in the Gulf of Mexico. I'm not going to tell you how much they invested with me, but to say that they had a "fat checkbook" is a major understatement. They knocked me off my feet; as I had never seen that many zeros before!

Now I didn't have just one East Coast investor. Eventually, I had sixteen, including the endowments of Yale, Duke, Wellesley, the State of Massachusetts, the University of North Carolina and other top-flight institutions. Other big deals closed with Harvard, including a major project with the Cullen family in Houston and other Texas wildcatters.

Oil and Gas Investor Magazine/Hot Dogs, Harry and Harvard
With Harry Cullen, one of the best wildcatters in the history of the business, in the late 1980s.

In 1960, this young man from Wharton, Texas, heard his father say, "If you want to be really successful, **work hard, be patient, stay focused** and head east to make your business dreams come true." Daddy would have been proud. It took me twenty six years, I listened to him and I did it. I never lost sight of my dream and worked night and day to see it come true.

So I'm a college dropout, but here's what I learned: Everyone has a dream. And those dreams can take you places **you might never imagine.**

I dreamed of success in the oil business: that one took twenty-four years. I dreamed of becoming a champion dancer: that one took me seven years. I dreamed of a beautiful life with my wife, my family and my friends: that one is a dream I am fortunate enough to live each day. Today, I dream about how all my years of hard work can benefit others long after I am gone.

Along the way, I learned keep your head down, work hard—really, really hard. Be patient and hang in there. Dream your dreams, and dream big. You might have to learn to eat a few hot dogs, but you can do it.

94

Whatever you want to accomplish in life is within your reach. Just give it the old Harvard try.

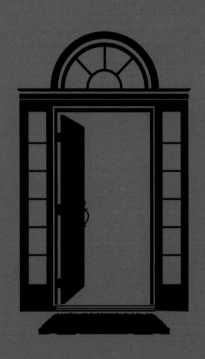

5

the puppy file

I am sure that there is some kind of **invisible target** on my back. Maybe it's a cardboard sign or much more likely, bright red neon lights that spell out **"GOT MONEY: ASK ME FOR IT."** Of course, subtlety is definitely *not* in my vocabulary so it's probably not just neon lights, but they are flashing in some kind of **disco rhythm,** too. I can just hear it now—Michael Jackson's "Don't Stop Till You Get Enough."

Now, don't get me wrong, **I go asking for it.** Gifts like The Smith Foundation's most recent grant for researching breast cancer through sequencing the human genome make a pretty nice headline *and* cause a beehive of buzzing activity in my mailbox.

Very deeply rooted in my philanthropy is something that anyone, and I do mean anyone, can do: *give* more than you take.

Sounds like something my Hebrew teacher might have said, but since I was too busy being the class clown to pay that much attention in class, maybe I heard it first from my father. I'm sure that Daddy never used those exact words, but he definitely spoke them loud and clear: his short life was marked much more by what he left behind than what he took.

And what he left behind for me, besides the humble sum of $500, was the gift of giving. And, as the commercial says, I believe it is a gift that keeps on giving.

It keeps on giving because—in the shortest of reasons—**IT FEELS GREAT.** You should try it. I myself have tried way too many things that make me feel great and this one takes the cake. Without incriminating myself, it is in fact the best high there is.

But it is so much more than feeling great. Giving your time, money, blood, an organ, an education, a place to sleep, a meal, a kind word—it has the power to transform both the giver *and* the receiver. I think my dad knew that. He knew what it felt like to make people feel welcome.

And he welcomed them all. From the new immigrant to Texas, to the new guy in

philanthropy:

Altruistic concern for human welfare and advancement, usually manifested by donations of money, property or work to needy persons; by endowment of institutions of learning and hospitals and by generosity to other socially useful purposes

He welcomed them all. From the new immigrant to Texas, to the new guy in the oil patch, my dad was eager **to lend a hand.**

the oil patch, my dad was eager to lend a hand. It seems there was always someone new at our dining room table in Wharton: the cousin of someone in New York eager to make a home in Texas, a neighbor whose husband was suffering from a terminal illness **and of course,** there were always extended family members joining us.

At about age six, I was out in the garage looking at our dog Lady's new puppies when I asked my father about yet another stranger in our house. He used an analogy that may seem odd.

"Daddy, how long is Mrs. Rosenberg going to be here?"

"As long as she needs to," my dad answered.

"But why is she here? **Doesn't she have a home?"**

"Yes, she does, about 100 miles south of here," he said. "Her husband is sick in the hospital here in Wharton, and she wants to be near him."

This still didn't seem very logical to me and as always, I persisted.

"But if she has a home, why doesn't she just go there? Why does she have to live with us?"

My dad stared at me and I could see that he was struggling to make me understand.

"Lester, do you see these puppies?" he asked pointing to the box. Inside were six brown balls of smooth fur. Lady was licking them.

"Those puppies have a home, but they still need someone to take care of them. You could say that Mrs. Rosenberg is like a puppy right now. She needs someone to care for her."

I couldn't imagine anyone licking Mrs. Rosenberg but it seemed like a good answer at the time. And from then on, every time I was introduced to a new guest in our home, I knew it was one of Daddy's "puppies."

When my father died in 1960 of a heart attack at the young age of forty-six, his office manager took my two brothers and me aside and showed us a big file cabinet. It was Daddy's Puppy File. Inside were tear-stained notes, letters and photographs of all the people he had supported in various ways. There was **page after page** of loans made, scholarships provided, gifts to extended family members and contributions to causes in our hometown and all the way to Israel. To an accountant, the balance sheet didn't measure up. And that's because he never expected anything in return. **The real return on his investment** was evident in all the notes and letters he had saved. These were Daddy's puppies, right before my eyes.

At my father's funeral, the rabbi used a Hebrew word to describe Daddy that I had never heard: **"chesed."** The wordsmith that I am not, I had to look up its meaning recently when I received a copy of the eulogy. In the best translation, its English equivalent is "loving-kindness," but other words are associated as well: mercy, goodness, love and beneficence. I had to look *that* one up, too. It means being kind, helpful and generous.

It was stunning to see one word that **defined him so well.** Others have described

Janet McCardy established a new primary and elementary school in Kenya in 2007 with funding from The Smith Foundation.

my father in terms that I snicker about. Believe me, he was no angel, a genetic code I certainly got from him.

But I am grateful for being on the receiving end of what matters most, and I remain in awe of how much I learned from him—in the oil business and in the business of giving. I know without a shadow of a doubt that my father gave much more than he took. I hope and pray that I can do the same. And that is why today, **I have my own Puppy File.**

My glowing, neon sign might need a new bulb or two, but I am working on it; it pales in comparison to the simple cardboard one that I am sure my dad wore his entire life. His simply read, "You're welcome."

6

caesar's story

Dreaming of Benihana

I don't like going to the office every day. But it doesn't mean I don't work. Actually, I am always *at* work no matter where I am. Armed with a Blackberry and my computer, I can pretty much work anywhere. And if you happen to be at home with a **drop-dead gorgeous wife,** it's nice to not have to rush to the office every morning.

Drilling oil wells and leasing mineral rights take a massive amount of paperwork, so we use a delivery service to transfer documents from my home office to the one downtown. I ask myself, **"Is this a good thing?"** I think it is, especially because if I had been downtown on June 9, 2004, I wouldn't have answered the door and met Caesar. It was like this:

The doorbell rings, I answer it and there stands a young man in his 20s.

"I have a delivery for Mr. Smith," he says. His eyes widen as I invite him in. "I'm Mr. Smith, but you can call me Lester," I tell him. "What's your name, son?" I ask him.

"Caesar," he answers.

Caesar stands there looking around the house, and I can tell he wants to see more. **"Would you like to take a look around?"** I ask him. Caesar nods and I show him around the house; he meets the dogs, and he really likes the pool. After the tour, I escort him back to the front door.

"Caesar, how long have you been working for the delivery service?" I ask.

"Mr. Smith, I have been delivering to your house for a long time. I have always wanted to meet you," he says. "Whenever my boss calls and says, 'Go to Mr. Smith's house,' I drop whatever I am doing."

"Tell me about you," I ask. **"Are you married?"**

Caesar opens his wallet and shows me a photo of him with a pretty young woman.

"That's my wife Teresa and my daughter," Caesar says proudly. "I met my wife in

108

initiative:

One's personal, responsible decision

Money is just like manure. It is best if spread around.

the 4th grade in Brownsville and told her I was going to marry her," he says. "She told me I was crazy, but I was patient," he added with a wink.

"I knew she wouldn't marry me unless I had a good job, so I came to Houston and started working and saving money," he says. "I finally convinced her to marry me when I was nineteen years old."

I learn that Caesar's father had been an illegal immigrant and had married his mother to get his residency. The family grew up in Brownsville, but **his father encouraged him** to move to Houston to find a better opportunity. He had dreams of going to air conditioning school; he and Teresa juggled work and parenting while she was attending nursing school.

I talk to Caesar a few minutes more and thank him for doing such a good job delivering my papers. I hand him three one-hundred dollar bills. I love giving big tips. You should try it sometime and see what happens. People usually say things like, "But I couldn't accept such a gift!" Or, "No, please, I shouldn't." Then I tell them to give it back. Generally they don't. People are funny that way. To the really stubborn ones I say, "Okay, you're right. I'm sorry I put you in such a difficult position; please forgive me." Then I hold out my hand for the bills. **No one gives it back.** At least no one ever did until Caesar.

Caesar stands there staring at those bills, speechless. I love watching the expression on his face. I know it is **a lot of money for a tip,** but I can really see that he is going to put it to good use. This young man has a wife going to college and a young daughter to support. I also learn that he often sent money to his relatives. With tears in his eyes, he hands the money back to me. "Thank you, Mr. Smith, but I can't take this," he says reluctantly.

"Yes, you can, Caesar," I say. "You have earned it. You see, I'm a busy man. I make my living drilling oil wells. If you didn't do a good job of getting these important documents to me, I wouldn't be able to do my job. So you can tell your boss that this is a tip from Lester Smith for a job well done."

I push the bills back into his hands.

"No, Mr. Smith, I just can't take this," he says. "No one has ever given me anything like this before. I don't feel right taking this money." He thrusts the notes back at me.

Caesar was one tough nut. This took some last-minute scrambling of my brain. How else could I persuade him? I needed a different approach.

"Caesar, you must be pretty busy driving a car during the day all day and taking care of your daughter when your wife is at school," I say. "Do you ever have time to go out with your wife, **just the two of you?"**

He shakes his head.

"We like to go dancing sometimes, but we are so busy and trying to save . . . ." his voice trails off.

Bingo!

With tears in his eyes, he hands the money back to me. "Thank you, Mr. Smith, but I can't take this," he says reluctantly.

"Well, Caesar, this gift is not for you, it's for Teresa," I say. "So you do something special for Teresa and have some fun. **Take her out;** go dancing, whatever she likes to do. You can tell her this is a gift from Mr. Lester Smith because her husband has done such a good job for me."

With a grateful smile, Caesar takes the money. Finally.

He looks at the bills and shakes my hand over and over again. I wish him luck and close the door.

A few weeks later, I was going through the mail when I saw a handwritten note. Those are the ones I absolutely love to receive. They really stand out in the piles and piles of funding requests and ball invitations that on most occasions end up in the trash. How many handwritten notes do any of us get these days? **Not enough.**

The card read: Thank You; Sharing a Little of Your Time Really Meant A Lot.

Inside was a note:

3-28-06

Dear: Mr. Lester Smith

I want to thank you for your generosity. I did just as you suggested, treated my wife to a nice dinner. Thanks to You I was able to fulfill her dream of going to Benihana. Once again, on behalf of my wife, daughter and myself,
        thank you.

Teresa Lopez

Arizbeth Lopez

(This is a photo of my family) at Benihana Restaurant.

Sharing a little of your time really meant a lot.

Please let me repay you and your wife by gratuitously working for you.

If you ever need any assistance personally or for your foundation, please do not hesitate to call me 24/7 at cell phone

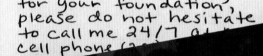

The Lopez family: Caesar, Teresa and daughter Arizbeth.

Included was a photo of **Caesar, Teresa and their daughter** at Benihana.

A few months later, I had the chance to see Caesar at the office. He began thanking me over and over again. I waved him off; I was hurrying to get into a meeting and was pressed for time. Then he said something that stopped me in my tracks.

"Mr. Smith, I wanted to tell you something that happened to my daughter," he said. "She just got her report card and it was all straight A's," he said proudly. "Thanks to you."

I didn't recall tutoring his daughter, but I listened.

"After we went to Benihana and I talked about you, my daughter wanted to know all about you—where you lived and what work you did. So one day when she was home from school, I took her to work with me."

Caesar described driving his daughter on his delivery routes and coming to my house and office. He described **her face when she drove up** and all the questions she asked.

"I told her that if she wanted to have a good life like yours and be able to help other people, she would have to study hard and make good grades," he says. "So now she is a straight-A student. **She wants to help people like you helped us.**"

Happily, Caesar's daughter has kept up her grades; she is in the gifted and talented program at her school, and she is on the honor roll. I take absolutely no credit for inspiring her to excel, but I am deeply touched that in some small way, **I have made**

116

a difference in that wonderful family's life and set one little girl on a new path.

In a city as large as Houston, it's easy to spot people like Caesar who have come to our country with big dreams of a new life and new opportunities. They are part of the very fabric of our city and often do the work most of us don't want to mess with, like driving a hot car, stuck in traffic delivering papers to some bald guy. If that were me, road rage would be way too polite to describe my mood. The majority are good people bent on one thing—work. **And they work hard, day after day.**

But these hard-working people are also easy to forget, or worse, ignore. I have often wondered what would have happened if I had not answered the door that day. I will tell you this: it still makes my day to recall my meeting with Caesar and even better, knowing how a few minutes of my time impacted him and his family. And even as I write this, I know with all my heart that it wasn't about the tip; it was about the time. The time that it took for me to stop yakking my head off and listen to his story.

I believe that everyone has a story. We are molded by certain experiences, both good and challenging, and the result is the timeline of our life. Caesar's story is just beginning. He's in the land of opportunity, and he will face setbacks and overcome the real challenges that we all inevitably face. Sadly, the biggest sting may be how he is treated by the rest of us bent on staying the course of our overly busy lives. But without **taking time to become engaged** with one another, be it partner, friend or the delivery guy, I think we lose sight of what it means to be kind and compassionate human beings. When we forget common courtesy and decency, we forget our own humanity.

So here's my challenge to you. Stop yakking and listen. Ask questions. Take an extra ten minutes out of your busy day to strike up a conversation with someone. The woman who pours your coffee at Starbucks. The kid who bags your groceries. The teller at the bank. A kind word, a job praised, even a sincere **"thank you"** will make their step lighter. I promise you, it will put a big smile on your face, too.

And if you can, give them a tip.
A really, crazy, big one.
And let me know if anyone
gives it back.

7

pay it forward

How The Smith Girls Became Oil Baronesses

It was the night of October 14, 2009, and I had been **up nearly all night** trying to birth an oil well in West Texas. My daddy always said that babies and oil wells are born at night, and my God, it sure seems that way.

Over the years I have drilled many wells in Texas, but this one was unique; I'm sure my memory of its birth will last me to the end of my days. And why? Because it was a pivotal moment when I learned once again **how great it feels** to pay it forward.

I have by far the most **dedicated, hard-working group** of people who work for me—some have been putting up with my crap for nearly twenty years. And during those twenty years, there were some great years,and there were many terrible ones as well.

By 2008, when the stock market crashed, it was a pretty hard time for everyone in my office. There were lots of long faces and retirement funds that had been decimated. The dollar was in a free fall against the other currencies of the world, and the only thing that made sense to me (which was pretty much my mantra all the years I'd been in business) was to keep the bulk of my wealth in hard assets, things that were tradable and needed throughout the world. **Oil fits that bill to a "T,"** and of course that's why they call it Black Gold. Now gold has a limited use, but oil is different; the world runs on oil. Although I had a big position in natural gas reserves, the production of those reserves mainly went to the domestic market and was therefore tied to the ups and downs of the U.S. economy, which was falling like a rock.

On the other hand, oil was priced in dollars and if the value of the dollar declined, the price of oil went up, great hedge for irresponsible fiscal policy. Hey, it's no secret I'm not a fan of Barack Obama. **I still miss Reagan,** I think General Schwarzkopf should get his keester out of retirement and back to work and the Bushes—41 *and* 43—are on my favorite hits album.

So what could I do for all of these women in my office—hard-working, dedicated, loyal and faithful, who had been through it all with me—the good times and the bad, in

dedicate:

To give or set apart entirely to a specific person, activity or cause

sickness and in health? Hell, it sounds like marriage! And in a way, it is. We're not joined in matrimony but in deep **respect, trust and yes, friendship.** I call these ladies my "office wives" and often, they even sheltered me like I was their small child. Twelve of them taking care of one really spoiled brat!

During my many brushes with illness, injuries and cancer, not to mention hundreds of dry holes, they prayed for me, they wrote me encouraging notes, they always smiled and said, **"Lester, it is going to be okay."** And you know what? They also did their jobs, running the office like a well-oiled machine. When I was going through chemotherapy, feeling like crap most of the time, short-tempered, scared to death, worried out of my mind, they were a constant source of support.

I wanted them to know how much I valued them for standing by my side—but how?

And one night, it became crystal clear. At least as clear as things can be at 2 A.M.

I sat straight up in bed and had an epiphany. And **this is what I heard** in my foggy head:

You know, Lester, these women have been your business partners for decades. Why not make them **partners** *in an oil well? You're sixty seven years old, and God willing, you have another twenty-plus years in you. You're only going to give the money away, because you can't take it with you.*

Then the little voice said . . .

124

Why not make them oil baronesses?

Oh my goodness, I was so excited I could hardly get back to sleep. I couldn't wait to see their faces. This was the perfect plan, and I couldn't wait to tell them. But all in good time. I just love a good scheme, and this one would **take the cake.**

With that in mind, I put the lawyers to work creating the documents that would mean a very different future for each of my office staff. I put up all the money and gave them a pretty good interest in the new well I was drilling out in West Texas. This was something I had never done—ever. And now looking back on it, I am so proud that I did, because it is my firm belief that good works start at home.

The excitement in the office while we were drilling that well was absolutely electric! Everyone—and I mean everyone—learned a new "oil field" language and began to experience the **highly charged emotions** of drilling a wildcat well. I would call them into the office with reports; one day it was good, the next day it was bad, and the following day looked pretty gloomy, too. It was an emotional roller coaster ride for them, but not for me. I was as calm and collected as ever because I had done this plenty of times. Since my seventh birthday. So in essence, everyone in the office was getting to relive that birthday over sixty years ago. This time I was the one handing out the presents and they were called **"financial interest."**

I was up all night nursing that well in, and I arrived a bit later than usual at the office the next morning. I called the staff in and put on my best long Lester face.

And one night,
it became crystal clear.
At least as clear as things
can be at 2 A.M.

"Well, I have some news to report about your well," I said flatly. You could have heard a pin drop. I relished this moment. "We hit a big one, ladies, **a real barn burner!"**

And when I say, "hit a big one," it was one of the better wells I have drilled in the past twenty years!

There were high fives, there were tears and there was screaming and hollering. My long-time assistant, Julie, was walking around with a sign posted on her lapel that read, **"Where's my check** so I can go to Neiman Marcus this afternoon?" The floor was lined with fake one-thousand-dollar bills leading to my geologist's office and continuing to my office. Music blared. It was like the president of the United States had walked into the office. **I felt like a million dollars.** Paul, our geologist, had been on the well all night and had just flown in. He was greeted like Caesar coming into Rome. It was like Christmas morning at Smith Interests.

At the end of that eventful day, the entire office was totally exhausted—the staff from joyous emotion and me from being up all night. What a great feeling it was for me to be there when they made their first well.

I did what I set out to do. I put them in the oil business. And I didn't just put them in any old well; I put them in a gusher!

About 6:30 that evening, after everyone else had left, I was sitting at my desk with a big smile on my face and decided **it was time to go home.** I was absolutely starving, and I realized I had forgotten to eat that day. My adrenaline had been flowing full blast for the past seventy-two hours. Famished, I got into my SUV and headed toward home. As is my custom, I stopped at the convenience store around the corner from my house.

I may have given up lots of vices in my life, but this was one vice that still had its hold on me. And like some of the other bad habits I have enjoyed in my life, this one, while legal, could still get me **in trouble with my wife** and my doctor.

So you will understand why I can *never* tell them about that convenience store. Okay, just promise you won't rat me out. They sell my two favorite food groups: **doughnuts and ice cream.**

Ah, just the sound of the word "doughnut" conjures up such love and devotion. Doughnuts and I have a very special relationship. And it's been going on for years.

You see, I had a heart attack when I was fifty-seven years old; my dad died of a massive heart attack at the young age of forty-six. You would think that **I would have known** to take better care of myself. But *nooooo* . . .

Each day on the way home from work, I would stop off and have a couple doughnuts and a cup of coffee. And my sweet wife, Sue, busted my butt every time.

I'd walk in the house and she'd ask, "Where have you been?"

I'd innocently reply, "Just driving home from the office, dear."

She would look at me and say, "You stopped and had a doughnut, didn't you?"

I would look at her very seriously and say "I did not have a doughnut!" And she'd

The Smith Girls. My Office Wives. The Oil Baronesses. They're the best!

say "Lester, you're lying to me. You had a doughnut."

"Look, I'm not lying. I really didn't have a doughnut."

"So what's that sugar on your chin?"

Busted again! How about busted every time I eat a doughnut? You would think at my age I would be smart enough to remove the telltale signs from my face. No, not me . . . just plain dumb, fat and happy!

I really got busted by my cardiologist, Dr. Lance Gould from the University of Texas Health Science Center. I was in for my annual checkup and found out that I had gained a few pounds since my last appointment—fifteen pounds to be exact, but who's counting? Well, he was.

The nurse put me on the scale, and as I recall, she said something like, "Good Lord, you've gained fifteen pounds, Mr. Smith! **What happened?"**

It was those damn doughnuts again. I explained about my little afternoon coffee break, and she wanted to know how many doughnuts I usually had. I generally respect people in uniforms; they usually mean business. I find it's harder to fib to them.

"I don't know, maybe one or two?"

She didn't believe me. I knew the look well.

"Okay, more like three or four," I admitted.

She wrote it all down in my chart with a "tsk" sound and then ordered me to remove my shirt and wait for the doctor.

So there I was, half naked, sitting in a cold office, when Dr. Gould came in. I swear this is exactly what he said. "Look at that fat belly hanging over your belt. I hear that you have been eating those chicken-shit, candy-ass doughnuts."

My mouth hung open. **Did he miss the "warm bedside manner"** class in medical school?

I looked at him and said, "Dr. Gould, I need to ask you a question."

"Is 'chicken-shit, candy-ass' a medical term?"

He was not amused.

"If you don't stop eating those chicken-shit, candy-ass doughnuts, you're going to have another heart attack."

So I quit. I did. For a long time.

But then, the lure of those fresh, sweet, doughy buns called me back to the dark side.

So back to the story at hand.

I pulled my black SUV into the store parking lot, burst through the double wide doors and was greeted by the round Pakistani manager just as he has greeted me for years.

"Hey, Mr. Doughnut Man!" he shouted.

"Hey, Mr. Pakistani Man!" I called back. "You still hustling customers for Lotto tickets?"

Oh, my, look at these beauties—they're all mine!

There were a dozen or so people standing in line to check out; they all turned to look at me.

I said, "Don't buy any Lotto tickets from him. I can't tell you how much money he's conned me out of."

Everybody laughed, and some of the regulars shared their stories about Mr. Pakistani Man.

As I was waiting in line, eager to get my sugar high going, I noticed a young boy standing by the display of hot food items, a crumpled five-dollar bill clutched in his hand. He was pacing back and forth, and I could see the indecision in his face. He was trying to decide how he was going to spend his five dollars. I could also see in his eyes that he wanted an after-school treat that cost more than he had.

Now me, I was feeling high as a kite. No drugs, no alcohol. **I was just high on life,** knowing that I had given the employees at Smith Interests their first oil well. I turned to the young man and said, "Buy anything you want. It's on me." He looked at Mr. Pakistani Man who nodded and said, "Mr. Doughnut Man means it. Get whatever you want."

We all had big smiles on our faces. He came back to the counter with cheese-covered nachos and a big burrito. He was skinny as a stick, so I had no idea where all that food was going to go. I gave Mr. Pakistani Man my credit card and found out I had just spent $10.72. After I paid, the young man looked at me and said just simply, "Thank you."

I said, "You're welcome, son. Now I want you to do me a favor. Go out and **do**

something nice for someone else."

As he walked out the door, there was another gentleman standing at the counter getting ready to check out. He asked Mr. Pakistani Man what had just happened.

"Mr. Doughnut Man here just bought that boy his dinner."

The guy waiting at the counter turned to me and said, "You know, God is going to pay you back tenfold."

I looked back at him with a big smile on my face and said, "Yeah, I know. He already has."

Still feeling like a million dollars, I hopped in my car, tried to remove all trace elements of sugar from my face and headed home. A car pulled up beside me. The driver's window came down and a hand motioned me to do the same.

A lady stuck her head out of the window. She said, "Thank you very much for what you did for my son." She stuck her hand out of the window; in her hand was the crumpled five dollar bill. She looked at me and said, **"Pay it forward."** I nodded, smiling broadly and soared home.

Like me, that mother and her son will never forget what happened on October 14, 2009. I will bet you a dollar to a doughnut hole that they will "pay it forward" again and again, and every time, they will tell that story.

My ten-dollar investment will reap more rewards than I can ever imagine. When you begin to see how little it takes to "pay it forward," you can do the same thing.

134

Mr. Pakistani Man and Mr. Doughnut Man

None of us has any idea of all the wonderful ways a single random act of kindness can perpetuate itself for years to come.

That evening I told Sue the story. Just as we turned out the lights I said, "Honey?"

"Yes, Lester?"

"Do you know what I'm going to do? I'm going to make **all those people** that work for me wealthy."

"I know you are, Sweetie."

"And you know what else?"

"Hmmm?"

"I am going to stop by the convenience store every day on my way home and pick up someone's tab."

"Just remember, Lester. **No doughnuts.**"

Busted again.

There was one last good-night kiss and all four of us—Sue and I and our doggies, Bucky and Sadie—curled up and slept as hard as rocks.

October 14, 2009, felt as thrilling to me as winning my first United States dance championship title had felt in 2002. How in the world does drilling a successful well have anything to do with dancing? There's an old saying: **"You dance with the one who brought you to the party."** Those girls in my office brought me to the party, and now I'm doing the jive with every one of them!

None of us have any idea of all the wonderful ways **a single random act of kindness** can perpetuate itself for years to come.

8

celebration

Some people are just **born to be president**—and some are born to be first lady. I have always been a great admirer of those who are called to such high office, and I am more so now that I have had a chance to **see one tinkle** and another tinkle with laughter.

I'm a big fan of President Bush, number 41. I think quite highly of 43 too. The Bush family is just about the closest thing to royalty that we have here on this side of the pond.

YOU GOTTA DANCE LIKE NO ONE'S WATCHING

I have never seen one of these rooms that I could pass up.

And while I have had the pleasure of meeting lots of famous people in my life, nothing quite prepared me for the circumstances under which I met and became friends with President George H. W. Bush.

Sue and I had been invited to sit in Bob McNair's sky box in Reliant Stadium to watch our hometown team, the Texans. Bob owns the team, and we had met as trustees of Baylor College of Medicine. Bob and his wife, Janice, are incredibly generous and two of the most outstanding people I know. I hope when they read this they'll invite me back to that sky box. But after my men's room escapade, they likely will want to forget my name.

Now, I can have a **pretty good conversation with a lamppost,** or so I'm told. But I admit when, during halftime, I dashed into the men's room and found myself standing at the urinal next to 41, I was a little tongue-tied.

I was so nervous I didn't know what to do or say. I mean, this was President Bush! Why hadn't I read the book on Presidential Urinal Protocol? I thought about extending my hand, but it was a little busy at the time.

Was it okay to speak to him in midstream? It seemed so disrespectful. And since I majored in saying the wrong thing at the right time, I was pretty sure that whatever I'd say would be totally inappropriate.

It's hard to remember all the thoughts that went through my bald head in rapid succession, but it went something like this:

Oh my God, I am peeing next to the president!

Oh my God, I think I have peed on my shoe, next to the president.

Oh my God, I hope he didn't notice.

Well, the president's aim was a lot better than mine, and no, he didn't seem to notice. Even if he did, he probably wouldn't say anything because that's what presidents do, I think: ignore someone who pees on himself.

We both finished our business and washed our hands, and that's when I made my big move. I said, "Hello, how are you?"

And the president said, "Fine, how are you?" And he walked out of the door. Pretty quickly, I might add.

From that moment on I told everyone who would listen that I was **close personal friends** with President Bush. Talk about being full of it—well, that's just me and what can I say?

If President Bush remembered my little **potty incident,** he didn't let on when we were introduced to one another at Houston's Celebration of Reading event. There I was with Sue, so nervous that he might recall my little "accident," when he described one of his own embarrassing moments.

During his presidency, he said, he was getting ready to deliver an important speech when an aide came over and whispered, **"Mr. President, your pants are unzipped."** To this he quipped, "Don't worry. An old bird never falls far from the nest!"

From that moment on I told everyone who would listen that I was close personal friends with President Bush. Talk about being full of it— well, that's just me and **what can I say?**

This was our first party in our home for Celebration of Reading,
supporting the wonderful literacy efforts of my good friend and "baby," Barbara Bush.

At that moment, I knew that any faux pas I might have committed would certainly be forgiven by a classy old bird like that. But leave it to me, there were still other Bush family members that I have managed to regale with inappropriate actions or comments. God help them, they're probably wondering how to get rid of me by now.

The old bird story was among the many great tales we have heard over the years at Celebration of Reading, established by Barbara Bush to raise funds for family literacy programs through the Barbara Bush Foundation for Family Literacy.

I have one word for those of you who have not attended this incredible event—*GO*.

On this wonderful evening, best-selling **authors give voice to their own books.** I hang on every word. But my favorite part of the evening is hearing first-hand how a student has learned to read—and how that life has been changed through the experience. Until I began attending Celebration of Reading, I had never considered that there are thousands of children and adults who lack basic literacy skills, even today. They don't know how to read a newspaper, fill out a job application or read a bedtime story to their children. Now, I strongly believe that when we provide opportunities that **teach people to read and comprehend,** we set them on a path of success otherwise unattainable. No, I am not on the board—remember I'm trying to get off boards these days—but I just believe helping people learn to read is an incredible gift that will change their lives forever. More than a gift. In fact, it is a responsibility for us to do whatever we can to make sure every child grows up reading.

145

Back in Wharton, I grew up in a family that loved to read. My favorite books were The Hardy Boys series, and my brothers and I would pretend to be boy detectives just like Frank and Joe. Of course, **I loved comic books** and had quite a collection of them too. They were in another old shoe box under my bed, next to my rock collection that was later replaced with magazines that my mother said would cause blindness if I stared at them too long. I told her I only wanted to look at them until I needed glasses. She was not amused. I can still taste the dish soap in my mouth.

Even though I hadn't spent much time reading my assignments during my short stint in college, as an adult, **I devoured local and national newspapers and fiction.** When my business grew, fiction was pushed aside by required reading of oil and gas journals and business publications. So you can imagine my absolute delight when I went to my first Celebration of Reading event at the Hobby Center in 2007. I was enthralled at seeing, hearing and even meeting some of the all-time great authors—and comedians. That year the authors included Karyn Frist; David McCullough and his daughter, Dorie McCullough Lawson; Nathaniel Philbrick and **funny man Bob Newhart.** He just cracked me up!

Our family foundation has always supported educational initiatives, and Sue and I have **personally funded dozens of scholarships** for family members and even total strangers. We've met kids working at Starbucks, trying to get into law school and waitresses in Colorado trying to finish college while raising families. I've met many

146

determination:

The act of coming to a decision or fixing or settling a purpose; the quality of being resolute; fixed direction or tendency toward some object or end

people at AA who are trying to get an education while turning their lives around.

I have seen that the key to educational success doesn't necessarily lie in academic scores. Rather, hard work and determination are critical; if you have those qualities, you will be successful. I was never an outstanding student, but I did know how to work hard and achieve my goals through **perseverance and determination.** And if I can do it, anyone can.

When the Celebration of Reading program ended, we were invited to sit with Mrs. Bush and Bob Newhart for dinner. Perhaps because Mrs. Bush makes everyone feel so comfortable, or perhaps because my former wife is also named "Barbara," or both, I disgraced myself once again with my lack of tact and poise.

As we were leaving, I turned to Mrs. Bush and said, **"Barbara, it was so nice** having dinner with you."

As the words tumbled out of my mouth, I was in shock that I had used her first name—I turned totally red and stammered, "I apologize, Mrs. Bush. **Barbara was my first wife's name** and it is very familiar . . ." She was so gracious and dismissed it with a smile. "Lester, you can always call me Barbara."

She made a big fan of me that night, that's for sure. And there have been many more opportunities since for me to make a complete fool of myself and to receive her forgiveness.

The Smith Foundation gradually increased grants to **Celebration of Reading,** and Sue and I have even hosted a couple events in our home to introduce others to this fantastic event. In 2008 we sat spellbound as authors Immaculée Ilibagiza, Jim Nantz, Kerri Goode-Gabriel, Amy Grant and the hilarious Jill Conner Browne (a.k.a. The Sweet Potato Queen) appeared on stage. Each year there is always some kind of big surprise; you never know what will happen because no one—and I mean no one— can find out in advance. Believe me, I have tried.

Well, during the 2008 Celebration the old presidential bird himself was up on stage when his cell phone starting ringing. He was so embarrassed. He apologized profusely, and we thought it was just one of those things that could happen to anyone, even a former president. It was "Bill" somebody, and no one thought anything of it until Mr. Bush said, "Let me put you on speakerphone." **Out walked President Bill Clinton,** who read from his book *Giving: How Each of Us Can Change The World.* Let me tell you, that was an unforgettable moment. We still feel fortunate that we were in the same room with such powerful, committed and smart people.

Clinton's book is the kind **I personally find appealing.** I love a task and all the better if it can make a positive difference in another's life.

I sat there in the audience thinking about all the ways I could change the world, and I realized that I had a story to tell, too.

I turned to Sue and said, "Honey, I'm going to write a book about my life experiences."

Sue stared at me blankly. This was the stare that said, "Yeah, right!", "Dream on" or maybe even, **"Are you out of your mind?"**

In her gentle, loving way she shot back, "But you can't write. And you sure as heck can't spell!" Now there were some encouraging words.

She certainly had grounds for doubting my wordsmanship. I was horrible at writing; the joke is I can't spell my way out of a wet paper sack. But I had spell check on my computer, so scratch that argument. Maybe I failed English—twice—but hey, that was a long time ago. I was certainly older and wiser, and of course I knew I could always hire a good editor. That would help.

Maybe it was an impossible task, but I love a challenge more than anything. Show me a barren patch of earth and I will show you oil. Show me the *cha-cha*, and I will win a dance championship. Show me a heart attack and a couple of bouts with cancer, and **I will show you a survivor.**

I just love impossible projects because . . . well, they are impossible. Hard projects take a while to complete; impossible ones just take a lot longer. I said, "Sweetie, why can't I write a book—it's just like dancing. All I have to do is practice and practice, and one day I'll get there."

"That's exactly how we won our **national titles for ballroom dancing,"** I continued. "Sheer hard work and determination. You just wait and see, I'm going to write a book and it is going to be a good one. You mark my words; one day I'll read to

Celebration of Reading reception 2010. What a wonderful couple.
kind, compassionate and loving. The Bushes are OK too!

Dancing the cha-cha with my star at the Ohio Star Ball in 2002.

you from my book. I promise you that."

As I thought through what I had just said, lingering doubts set in.

Well, Lester, you did it again. You opened your big fat mouth and inserted your foot.

Sure, he can dance and drill wells, but can he write?

The short answer is "no." Some people are great at foreign languages, some win national spelling bees and some become great orators and statesmen, but not Lester Smith. I can't write, but I've always loved to spin a yarn. I knew my challenge would simply be putting my stories into written form. That's right, Lester the writer was born.

Now numbers are a completely different story. They call me Rain Man at the office. Great at counting cards in Vegas and great with numbers—that was Dustin Hoffman and that is me.

What I lack in formal education, I make up for in **chutzpah.** Here we are with a short book of my life stories. You know what? I have loved every minute of the process. Taking time to go back through the stories that have created my life has been a complete joy. If nothing else, I hope it will serve as a reminder to my grandchildren that their Pops was willing to take a few risks, even in the face of daunting self-doubts and criticism. And if I can get them to take a few risks and forge ahead with their own dreams, then all my late-night ramblings and rememberings will have been worth it. And that's all the literary success I need.

Following the program, Sue and I had the pleasure of sitting at dinner with President Bush, who is perhaps as well known for his tear ducts as he is for early departures. After passing Sue the large cookie tray and urging her to try each variety, the former commander in chief looked at me and said, **"Lester, aren't you getting tired?"**

"No, I feel just fine, Mr. President," I answered. Was he kidding? Google "night owl" and my image will come up, I swear.

He persisted.

"But Lester, don't you have to go to work early tomorrow morning? Won't you be *really* tired in the morning if you don't go home right now?"

He winked.

Finally, I got it.

I said, "Mr. President, I hate to leave your company and this wonderful event, but I have an early meeting tomorrow and I really must get home."

Before the words were out of my mouth, President Bush slapped his hands down on the table, stood right up and loudly said, "Folks, I have to go. I have an early meeting in the morning." And with that, he came over, shook my hand and patted me on the back . . . and he left.

We had come a long way from the men's room at Reliant Stadium.

In 2009 the line-up of authors for the Celebration was incredible. It included Pulitzer-Prize winner Jon Meacham, Cherie Blair, Christopher Buckley, Ted Bell and

154

chutzpah:

Unmitigated effrontery or impudence; gall; audacity; nerve

Julia Reed. As each of them read from their books, **I was captivated.**

I always loved the **banter between President and Mrs. Bush,** and that evening was no different. But this evening, we were all looking at Mrs. Bush not as the tough former first lady but as a very beloved wife, mother and grandmother who had recently undergone heart surgery. Under the circumstances, those of us in the audience wondered what kind of surprise might be in store. There were indeed some big ones.

One surprise was a little piggy that visited the stage and left a calling card. Oinking on cue, he was a reminder of Mrs. Bush's recent heart surgery which had replaced a valve with one donated by a pig. But the biggest surprise came in the form of a baker's dozen of Bush grandchildren. They saluted their "Ganny" with precious stories that had every one of us teary-eyed—even Mrs. Bush. President Bush was beaming through his own tears. I thought, "After six decades of being married, he still adores his wife. How wonderful is that?"

Following the program, my daughter and I sat next to Mrs. Bush. Sue was at home with our dear little dog Maggie, who was sick with cancer. A dog lover herself, Mrs. Bush was kind and concerned about our Maggie; **she even sent us a note** when she heard of Maggie's death soon after. Her upbringing and her years of being first lady, an ambassador's wife and the spouse of a congressman **serve her well.** She never forgets names, she is totally engaged in what *you* are saying and she asks *you* questions.

To me, that's the stuff of love affairs—to have someone totally listen and pay

"No, I feel just fine, Mr. President," I answered. Was he kidding? Google "night owl" and my image will come up, I swear.

attention to little ole Lester. Yep, I'd say she has my number.

I am positive Mrs. Bush has never put her foot in her mouth. That may not be true of her husband, if the famous words of the late Ann Richards about being "born with a silver foot in his mouth" have any truth.

They could both take some lessons from me, however, if they ever wanted to really put their foot in it. I am really, *really* **good at putting my foot in my mouth.** I think I could teach a course on it: *Lester's Guide to Tactless Blundering for Dummies.*

I gave one lesson that night.

I sat right next to Mrs. Bush. We had such a wonderful evening together, it was as if we had been old friends forever and there was no one else in the room. I was totally smitten with her charm and *joie de vivre*. She is the kind of grandmother everyone wishes they had—wise and worldly, yet down to earth. I felt like I could ask her anything and she would tell the truth—and **not some watered-down version.**

As the evening ended, I got up, **gave Mrs. Bush a kiss on the cheek** and said, "It's been nice being with you, baby." Just at that moment, there was this suspended, out-of-body experience. I needed the dramatic rescue of a Ted Bell novel or the prayers of Amy Grant. I needed the perfect prose of Christopher Buckley or the miracle of Immaculée Ilibagiza.

"Oh my God. I cannot believe I said that."

My daughter came to the rescue.

"Mrs. Bush, I apologize that my father is flirting with you."

And without losing a beat, Mrs. Bush answered with a laugh, "He's not flirting with me; **I am flirting with him.**"

What a lady! What a night! I realized it had been a year since I decided to write a book and I was more inspired than ever. It was time to stop talking about it and actually write it. There's a big difference between saying and doing. There's a big difference in the **"saying" part and the "doing" part.**

The doubts came back: *how can a guy like me that never graduated from college and barely got out of high school because of his terrible grades ever conceive of writing a book? How could a guy who had no formal dance training say, "One day I am going to be a national champion?"* But then I heard a louder voice.

I figured if I applied the same principles to writing as I applied to dance—practice, practice and more practice, hard work and never giving up—that someday I would get that book written.

So I wrote when no one was watching, just like I had danced when no one was watching.

No one saw how many times I tripped over my own feet trying to learn to dance. No one saw how many nights I stayed up trying to find the right words to type or agonizing over another fall from social grace. I kept working and eventually got it done.

faux pas:

*a socially awkward
or tactless act*

So don't wait a year between saying and doing. Stop making excuses and do what you want to do. Stop the self-defeating chatter in your head, set **a goal or two, and do it.**

9

wag more, bark less

Bucky, Sadie and Maggie have provided **the most real, albeit canine,** examples of how to live life in the present. From the moment I get up in the morning to the end of my day, my four-legged family members are ever-present, **living life like there truly is no tomorrow.** They know when to eat, when to go out, when the mailman comes and when Sue and I are not at home.

YOU GOTTA DANCE LIKE NO ONE'S WATCHING

They also know when we pull the suitcase out to go on a trip. We can always find those little rascals sitting in our luggage with this sad look on their faces saying in dog talk, **"Don't forget about your puppies."** They don't worry, they don't talk back and their only goal in life is to please their masters. Smart? Just say the word "cookie" and see what happens. Yes, they have trained *me* quite well. Most of all, they have trained me to live right now, this very minute, not yesterday, for that is just a memory, and not tomorrow, for that is only a dream. Perhaps that is the secret to a truly happy life.

To live a dog's life used to sound really foolish when I was younger, but now that I am older—and I think wiser—it makes all the sense in the world. I think Sue loves Bucky, our precious rescue dog, more than me. So I have started signing my love texts to her: *I Love You, Bucky Sr. (That would be me, your adoring and adorable husband!)*

Anyone who has ever loved a pet will tell you that you feel their love and sadly, their loss as much (dare I say it—sometimes even more) as the loss of some family members. The plethora of books and movies depicting that unique and unwavering bond is a testament to the millions of animal fans whose lives would be undoubtedly lonelier without their furry, winged or scaly friends. Who can forget Lassie? Or the classic boy-and-his dog flick *Old Yeller*? I remember seeing it in 1957 at the movie theatre in Wharton. I think I still hold the town record for Most Tears Shed While Watching a Movie. **I was a wreck.** I couldn't wait to get home to our dogs, Freckles and Junior.

It is very difficult to put into words how attached I have been to my dogs since I was a child. I remember Lady gave birth to her puppies in the large drainage pipe that ran under our driveway. It was a miracle of life that left a huge impression on me. I watched for hours as **she licked each puppy clean and nursed them;** I can still hear their little whines and yelps, not to mention that fresh puppy smell. Once you've smelled that clean, earthy musk, you'll never forget it whether you're five or ninety-five.

My sweet four-legged darlings have always been there for me and my family. Through rain and shine, through good and bad, up and down, they always have been there to provide a mountain's worth of cheer in the form of a wet lick on the face. That lick says that everything's going to be all right. And it is. I believe it with all my heart.

The correlation between my antics and those of the canine variety are legendary in my circle. I am well known for going into someone's home, and first thing, getting down on the floor and **giving their puppy a big belly rub,** a tug at the ears, a wrestling match or a scratch on the back. Not only does it bring a big smile to my face, the dog loves it and the owners adore the attention their baby gets.

And why? Because we love our pets with all our hearts; dogs especially are wired for the same level of affection. They are pack animals and want—or even need—to be part of a family. Their very existence is tied to our own. They are bound by trust, loyalty and uncritical attachment—how many people can you describe in the same terms? I read somewhere that dogs just think of us as unusually shaped dogs. Can't you just hear

This is Bucky, who is just like me. We have great personalities—but, sometimes, we bite!

them now? **"Hey, Fido, what's up with the bald guy?** Fleas or mange? Plus he smells like he has been rolling around in a puddle of oil. His mommy needs to get him to the cleaners right away."

It's said you can judge people by how well they treat children and animals. Since I adore them all, I feel pretty good on all counts. The key is getting down on your knees and meeting them eye to eye—or nose to nose as the case may be.

The first thing I do when I see my grandchildren is ask them, "Do you want to play with Pops or do you want to play with Little Lester?"

Pops, of course, is their grandfather, the man who talks and acts like an adult and the one who hands out commands when necessary. "Go to bed, brush your teeth and eat your brussels sprouts."

But Little Lester is an entirely different person. He is my six-year-old alter ego who can be just as mischievous, fun-loving and carefree as any child. The grandchildren love their Pops, but they go crazy rolling around on the floor with Little Lester playing a game we call "Cats and Dogs." We bark and howl and run around on all fours chasing one another. Talk about freedom, talk about love and talk about the greatest memories we have of simply playing together and acting silly. Sometimes **we grown-ups forget how to act silly.** But if you have children or grand-children, try it! Don't worry about what anyone will say, because you have permission to just be a kid again. And your greatest reward will be the squeals of laughter that will linger in your heart forever—and theirs too!

In 1984, when I was first diagnosed with aggressive bladder cancer, **my dear childhood friend Bobby Weisz** and his wife, Harriet, came to my home to pay me a visit. I had just gotten out of the hospital after undergoing surgery to remove a tumor the size of a plum from my bladder. God must have been watching out for me because the cancer had not spread. It took many more rounds of surgery and even more rounds of chemotherapy during the next seventeen years to keep the cancer from spreading. Bobby said, "Well, Lester, it looks as if God has given you a second chance." With that, he presented me with the most beautiful golden retriever puppy I had ever seen. We both had tears in our eyes. Bobby asked, "What are you going to call your new baby?"

Without hesitation I said, **"I'm going to call him 'Second Chance'."**

We shortened his name to Chance, and that guy would lay in bed with me and look at me with those deep brown eyes for hours. I am convinced he knew I was hurting, and he was there to help nurse me back to health.

When I was sick with cancer, shaking from drugs or fear, Chance was **just what the doctor ordered** to feel better in a hurry. I am absolutely confident that there is no better medicine, or no better therapy, than a dog licking your face. Having been under general anesthesia more than forty times in seventeen years, a sort of ritual evolved when I got home from the hospital. I wanted Chance by my side. Later, after

second chance:

*An opportunity to repeat
an initial instance*

he was gone, it was Sadie and Bucky, along with a good dose of matzo ball soup, and cookies-and-cream ice cream. Simple pleasures were my medicine.

I marked my recovery with short walks, first to the mailbox, then down the street and finally around the block, with Chance by my side. I could almost hear him cheering me on, **"C'mon Lester, one more block, you can do it!"**

Chance died when he was eight years old, and I cried for six months straight. I loved him with all of my heart, and he was there for me 100 percant of the time—never asking for anything and always giving me his unconditional love.

Many years later the same familial glue binds Sue and me to our four-legged family members. We are absolutely crazy about our babies, our dogs, Bucky, Sadie and Maggie, and our two cats, Baby and her best feline friend, Ellie. Sadie is the only purebred. She's a sixteen-year-old Lhasa apso, who is now the little-old-lady Queen Alpha Dog of the house. We rescued the other four from the SPCA or CAP, wonderful organizations that help thousands of neglected, abused or homeless animals. Or perhaps I should say those four found us.

Our pets are as old as dirt. We joke that the real name of our home is the Smith Geriatric Home for Pets. God bless their sweet souls. Many a friend has said that when their time comes, they want to come back as one of our dogs. That's okay with me, as long as they like a good belly rub.

We rescued Bucky nearly eight years ago. I truly think God sent him to me to teach

Many a friend has said that when their time comes, they want to come back as one of our dogs. That's okay with me as long as they like a good belly rub.

me a few things; **Sue says he's just like me.** He has a great personality—he bites. That's me, alright! And sometimes you just don't know where he's coming from. One minute, he loves you all over, the next minute, you are getting the iodine. Recently someone was at our house and reached down to pet Bucky. I said, "Don't do that, he'll bite you." And guess what? He bit the tar out of that fellow, right on his thumb. Out came the alcohol and a Band-Aid and he said, "You told me, but I didn't listen." Bucky has had back surgery, and he still has two injured discs. Given his history of physical abuse and neglect, his biting is to be expected.

Next we rescued the cat, Baby, from the SPCA. Sue and I were looking at all those beautiful animals, and Baby stuck her paw out of her cage, motioning for us to come and get her. **We're well trained, aren't we?**

We adore our pets because they keep us alive and kicking and feeling young. There are hundreds of studies that illustrate the benefits of pet ownership, especially for the elderly. And I suppose since I can now collect social security, I fall into that category. If the walker fits . . .

These little creatures teach us to be patient, playful and forgiving. They model loyalty, attentiveness and a healthy lifestyle: eat only until you are full; take a nap every day; stretch before rising. And they teach us to be kids again. **Who doesn't love a joyride,** head hanging out and tongue wagging in the wind? My dogs get the biggest kick out of seeing me do that.

172

Bucky's precious face!

Bucky, Sadie and Daddy. We're going someplace, and we love our Daddy!

Not only have our animal companions taught us about living, **they have also taught us plenty about letting go.** Especially Maggie.

Our precious Maggie. We miss her so much.

We found the tiny creature roaming our neighborhood. She was filthy and suffering from numerous assaults on her little body; her back was full of BBs where she had been shot. The moment we saw her, we saw her spunk for life and a sweet disposition that her obvious abusive environment had not been able to destroy. We couldn't wait to get her home, that is to say, after a trip to the vet and groomer. She was like a miniature Afghan hound—with beautiful honey-colored hair that swept the floor. We posted signs, put ads in the paper, but no replies. We learned from the veterinarian that Maggie had been on the streets for some time, and I recall the vet thanking us for rescuing her. It didn't seem to register as much then as it does now. Rescue and transform is exactly what we did for Maggie and her furry friends, but when I look back on her life, **rescue and transform is what she did for us.**

One day after Maggie had been with us for several years we noticed that she was not her usual chipper self. Upon investigation, we noticed a bump on her back we had not seen before. After a trip to the vet, our worst fears were confirmed. Maggie had cancer.

Despite a battery of treatments, her cancer required surgery that involved removing her tail. Several weeks later, when **she wagged her "stubby"** for the first time,

Sue was in tears. Our dear vet prepared us in the best way possible, but we already knew our time with Maggie was drawing to a close.

In the spring of 2009 we gathered around our bed to say goodbye to Maggie. Sue and I held her close, **wrapped in her favorite blanket,** stroked her little frail body and whispered her name over and over. We told her how much we loved her and would miss her. The vet administered the drugs and she died in our arms. It was one of the saddest days of our lives, and all of us wept like our hearts would break. And in fact, our hearts did break a bit. No amount of time, money, love, affection or sheer determination could help her live. But when it was her time to go, she only had to look around to see how she had transformed our lives.

Maggie **brought us to our knees,** whether she was playing with her favorite toys or rolling around on the floor in our little ritual at the end of the day. And now there we were, on our knees once again. This time, it was not to play catch or tug-of-war but to whisper a last "we love you."

Isn't that how we all want to leave this world—surrounded by our favorite humans, telling us funny stories about things we did, reminding us not to be afraid, promising us they will protect us no matter what and whispering sweet words in our ears?

So, here's what I have learned about life from dogs. And it's true for other family members, too. **Wag more and bark less.** Even if you're a big dog, never be afraid to get down on your knees. Play. Throw a ball, bark and howl. Act like a kid

Isn't that how we all want to leave this world—surrounded by our favorite humans, telling us funny stories about things we did, reminding us not to be afraid, promising us they will protect us no matter what and whispering sweet words in our ears?

Sadie and Bucky with their true love—and mine—Sue.

and laugh till your belly hurts. Not only will dogs love it, your kids and grandchildren will too. Welcome wet kisses and cold noses, long walks and naps, and yes, lie down with the kids and animals now and then. Hold them and tell them how much they mean to you and how much you love coming home to them. And if you must use words, use **kind words, words that encourage and make their tails wag. Even if it is just a stubby.**

Do you want to watch me wag my stubby?

10

it's all about the numbers

As I came out of anesthesia in November 2001, my first thoughts were, **"Did they get it all?"** Actually, to be honest, my first thoughts were, "How long before I can pee again?" Yes, there were other physical urges that I was deeply concerned about, but frankly, with a custom bladder made from my large intestine already in place and just coming out of surgery for prostate cancer, there was only one way to spell R-E-L-I-E-F: I needed to know that, please God, **the rest of the plumbing would work, too.**

YOU GOTTA DANCE LIKE NO ONE'S WATCHING

This awakening marked the fortieth time since 1984 that I had been under general anesthesia for cancer and other health challenges. **When you have cancer, it is truly all about the numbers.** There are stage zeros, ones, twos, threes, and fours. I never could figure out why a stage zero was actually a cancer stage according to the American Cancer Society. At least in my bald head, that one seems illogical. It means "carcinoma in situ," which is Latin for "cancer in its place." In other words, it hasn't spread. If that is the best number, you can guess what the bad boy number is. Basically the numbers tell you how serious the cancer is. But you know what? It's all serious so don't kid yourself. You got a zero? Yippee. You still have "The Big C."

To all cancer patients, **the numbers are critical.** And for me, I learned just how important the numbers were while hanging out in the waiting room at the urology clinic. Every man there could talk PSA numbers like they were fluent in some urological foreign language. A PSA (prostate specific antigen) test measures the amount of PSA in the blood. Your score determines your risk for prostate cancer.

And believe me, those numbers are important and meaningful. They give you something to understand, **to deal with.** You know, like taking a math or science test in grade school. Only in this exam, you don't want to make a high score. You want to flunk.

There is something really encouraging when the doctors say, "Your numbers look good." Of course, I really like to hear that instead of, "Your numbers are off the charts."

patience:

An ability or willingness to suppress restlessness or annoyance when confronted with delay

This one snuck up on me, unannounced and definitely uninvited.
"The Big C" is a sneaky bastard.

Tell me that when we're talking barrels, not PSA scores. No, the doctor didn't say that, but that's what I was hearing when I first had signs that something wasn't working right.

When I had my first PSA test back in 1984, my score was 1.8. Pretty darn good. But in 2001 my score shot up to 4.2. How was I to know that it was not so good? Especially because for the last seventeen years I had been in the fight of my life battling bladder cancer. This one snuck up on me, unannounced and definitely uninvited. The "Big C" is a sneaky bastard.

But as I learned, the first PSA score isn't that useful; what's really, *really* important is how it changes over time. So when I went back ninety days later and found out that my PSA level was 11.8, it was time to call in the troops. Like many—too many—men, I did not know what the numbers meant. But the look on my doctor's face was hard and serious; it spoke volumes. He used the word "worrisome" and to this day, when I hear it, I get a cold chill. **I hate that word.** That is not a word you want your doctor to use—ever.

Subsequent tests revealed that I had highly aggressive prostate cancer and it had spread outside of my prostate to my pelvic nerve. I underwent surgery to remove my prostate, the nerve, my bladder, and God knows what else they took out and threw in the trash can. **Basically I had been gutted.**

After the surgery my doctor told me that there would be an 87 percent chance that

I would be cancer-free within five years. **There were those numbers again.** But those were pretty good odds, and I was sure willing to take them. I mean, what choice did I have?

So I had a major 100,000-mile overhaul. Take out the prostate and nerve, get a new bladder. Tires rotated and balanced, oil change and grease job. Washed and waxed and ready to go another 100,000 miles. "You can pick it up at 3:00 P.M. today, Mr. Smith."

I may not have graduated from college, but I consider myself reasonably smart. But smart doesn't help against cancer. There are tens of thousands of smart men—hundreds of thousands probably—who ignore the warning signs and don't get a simple blood test to determine their PSA score. You know why? Because many just don't want to know. **It's "worrisome," as the good doctor said.**

Now, it's easy for me to say, "Don't worry." But if you are like me, you will.

I am a worrier by nature and by religion. Jews are great worriers. Catholics too. Not to mention the guilt. When God was passing out worry and guilt, I must have been in line twice. I thought I was in line for a super-full-size head of hair. And now with a shiny cue ball for a noggin, I guess I got my lines mixed up.

Yep, God, I'll take a full order of worry with two sides of guilt.

You want fries with that?

After the **"worrisome" episode** I was so rattled that I nearly decked another patient in the waiting room.

Sue was sitting next to me, very upbeat, poised and positive. I was a sniveling basket case. A man leaned over.

"Hey, Lester, what's your score?" he asked. We had obviously met before, but I could not place him.

But what I heard was, "Hey, Lester, did you score?"

I was sure this old coot was looking at Sue with some leery expression, and of course, why not—she's a knockout. I was about to make some kind of ballsy retort when Sue leaned over and said, "He asked about your PSA score, Lester." Sue knows me so well. I began learning more about my PSA.

PSA scores are like magic numbers. And every guy needs to know his score. So if you are a guy, or if you care about one—your father, brother, son, uncle, grandfather, neighbor, *anyone* over fifty years of age—encourage them to get tested. And if there is a history of prostate cancer in the family, get tested earlier.

I was **shocked to learn** how many men—from oil executives to oil well workers—did not know how important it was to find out their risk factors for prostate cancer. It's only a simple blood test.

So guys—this is for you. If you haven't done it already, get off your butt, pull your head out of the sand and go get tested. If you are over fifty, experience any painful urination, can't pee or need to get up in the middle of the night to pee, call your doctor today. For the love of all you hold dear, do it. Do it for your wife or girlfriend, do it for your kids and grandkids, do it because you want to score again. And that brings me to a very important point. **When you catch prostrate cancer at an early stage, you can still enjoy a fabulous sex life. And if you don't believe me, ask my wife. She's still smiling, too.**

Sue and I were all smiles for many reasons—I was alive, we were (and are) head over heels in love, and we were dancing like there was no tomorrow. Pure joy!

11:

honor your father

Anything Worth Doing is Worth Overdoing

A neighborhood holiday party had just ended and several of us were enjoying a last glass of wine (that would not be me) and **spirited conversation (that would be me),** when a good friend asked about my most recent "C word" episode.

My recent dance with prostate cancer had been like being hit by a **lightning bolt on a clear day.** No warning, no red flashing lights, no Big Voice from Heaven, no nothing. It was subtle, just like a sledge hammer whacking me upside the head.

YOU GOTTA DANCE LIKE NO ONE'S WATCHING

By this point, I had gotten comfortable talking about cancer by the numbers—stages and PSA levels. But it's interesting to note the difference between a man asking another man about **his male body parts** and a woman asking a man about the same parts. And unlike that hilarious Wendy's commercial from days gone by, "Parts is Parts," at least *my* body parts are not all the same parts. I think most men would agree. Especially when we are referring to the main part. Let's face it, when the magic wand loses some of its, well, magic, it's not an easy pill to swallow.

Don't even think about **messing with my "stuff"**! Hey, that is what makes me a man. Take that away, and I'm a real zero, a nobody. Or so I thought.

With prostate cancer you don't just lose part of your stuff—you can lose all of your stuff. And efforts to save it, or its function, begin to take on a life of their own.

I wondered about this aloud to my concerned neighbors. All the men nodded in agreement. The women just looked at me like I was growing another bald head. No pun intended, I swear.

"Big deal," a neighbor said. "You're fifty-nine years old. What's so important about sex at your age?"

Was she freaking kidding me?

To tell you the truth, I have been known to go as long as two to three minutes without thinking about sex. And that was on a slow day.

"What's so important?" I asked. "Jeez, you just don't get it."

your stuff:

That part of the male anatomy that has countless euphemisms and contributes mightily to procreation and romance

Hey, that little fellow has been my very best friend since I was thirteen years old. I don't even want to begin to tell you how much trouble we have been in together. He was my steady companion when no one was there to comfort me. **And he never let me down.**

(And I think she really *didn't* get it, **if you know what I mean).**

Here's what I wanted to say: *Hey, that little fellow has been my very best friend since I was thirteen years old and I don't even want to begin to tell you how much trouble we have been in together. He was my steady companion when no one was there to comfort me. And he never let me down.*

I would elaborate here but that would be another story. No, another chapter. No, another book.

They all stared at me, eyes wide.

"It seems to me that as a society, we don't like to talk much about prostate cancer," I said. "We talk about skin cancer, we wear pink ribbons for breast cancer awareness and we tell our kids not to smoke so they won't get lung cancer."

I was on a roll . . .

"I mean, the fact is there are six men in this room. If statistics are true, one of you will be diagnosed with prostate cancer. You're all at risk."

Not to mention that their risk factors were increased because they were all long in the tooth.

Yes, the percentage is small—about 16.666 percent—but let me tell you guys this: if you are one of the unlucky ones, then it is 100 percent. Guess what? You're it; you've been tagged. What are you going to do now? Oh, I would guess you're going to do the same thing I did—roll up in a little ball, pull the covers over your head and **cry and**

cry and cry. Cancer is a very scary word, but it is especially scary when you are IT. That's all you can think about, every waking moment of the day, and that's all you dream about all night long as you pray into your pillow, "Please God, make it go away."

I looked at my friends and asked, "Do you know what your PSA level is, Bob? Stephen, do you know how to get tested for prostate cancer? Tim, did you know that every three minutes a man in the United States is diagnosed with prostate cancer?"

I couldn't stop. I had a soap box, and I was the only sober one in the room. Plus I was blocking the door so no one could escape.

"I wonder what it would take to raise the level of concern and awareness for prostate cancer, much in the same way we all wear pink ribbons for breast cancer."

My friend Jan Carson, a former local news anchor, looked at me and said, "Money."

Duh. Really?

"Okay, Jan, let's do it," I said. "Let's start a campaign for prostate cancer."

Jan looked at me, trying to read me. **No, I hadn't been drinking;** I gave that up years earlier. Yes, I was serious. And I was ready to put my money where my mouth was.

A couple days later, we met for four hours and mapped it all out. We didn't have to overcome some of the **biggest hurdles** in launching such a campaign because the Smith family had agreed to underwrite all costs—from office space and computers, to staffing, website design and all the paper goods associated with fund-raising and

196

awareness. It takes a lot of paper, especially the green-back kind. And to really put some weight to the campaign, Sue and I agreed to **match all funds raised** so that every dime would go directly to research. It all sounded great, but it needed a name.

I am not very clever with big words. You already know that if you've gotten to this point with me. But I am good at short words and phrases. Sounds and grunts I do quite well actually. Must be my caveman mentality. Whatever the reason, I am much better at single- or double-syllable words. I can do three, but four-syllable words put my brain on a double-spin cycle. I said the name of our campaign had to be simple. **Easy to read, easy to grasp.** It had to explain the mission, it had to be representative of our cause and of course, it could not already be in use.

Who was I kidding? I wracked my bald head for days.

Jan and her husband, Tim Connolly, a successful Houston businessman, came up with some great names, but I had to take the list to the members of The Smith Foundation board, Bucky, Sadie, Maggie and Baby. A vigorous tail wag, a certain bark or meow was the key, and of course, the promise that any funds I would donate would not negatively impact their cookie supply. Sue and I are very well versed in animal talk, so of course we understood their enthusiasm immediately.

What a **dedicated board that served on The Smith Foundation—** not to mention those great board meetings! We would all get on the floor in the master bedroom closet and roll around with plenty of belly rubs. We would always come up with a **unanimous decision.** "Whatever you want, just keep rubbing my belly," Bucky would bark. And the best part—I always got my way. So what else is new?

"What do you think of this one—*Prostate Cancer Kills*? Not one wag. Too harsh for their sensitive ears.

"How about *Houston Prostate Cancer Awareness Foundation*?" They yawned.

Hmmm . . . this was a tough audience. I saved the best for last.

The Honor Your Father Campaign for Prostate Cancer Research? Lots of tail wagging going on. **We nailed it.** Actually, Tim nailed it; it was his great idea and one of many outstanding contributions he and Jan made to get the campaign started on such a strong note. Of course Bucky, the only male in the house besides me, wanted to know his risk factors too, so I had to give him extra cookies and promise to tell him his PSA score at the next vet visit.

And that is how the **Honor Your Father Campaign** was born.

Jan Carson, who lost her father to the disease, headed the team as campaign chair. She is not only my dear friend, she is also one of the hardest-working women I have ever known. In record time Jan assembled an office and a staff and organized a strategy to put prostate cancer on the minds of Houstonians.

In addition to earlier commitments to Baylor's urology programs, The Smith Foundation pledged an additional matching gift to the *Honor Your Father* campaign.

The Baylor Partnership, the volunteer advocacy group at Baylor College of Medicine,

unanimous decision:

The passing of judgment on an issue under consideration with complete assent by all involved; being in complete accord

joined us in our mission by adopting prostate cancer awareness as its fund-raising project. **It was an easy sell:** you raise a dollar and The Smith Foundation will match a dollar. And we would do this by presenting a year-long series of events and fund-raising opportunities including a golf tournament and a gala with the entire campaign ending on Father's Day 2005.

We had some heavyweights behind the campaign, too. In addition to Jan and Tim, were Jan and Dan Duncan, one of the nation's most philanthropic couples, who served as campaign co-chairs. Like me, Duncan was a survivor of prostate cancer, and an oil and gas man to boot. He was truly one of the most generous, kind and humble men I have ever known, and I miss him to this day. I will always remember something he once said: "True wealth is really measured in the lives you touch, not in the dollars you have." And it's true. I am still working on growing up to be like him. For me, the humble part only works because of Humble Oil—it's our only shared vice.

But we also shared the devastating news of a cancer diagnosis, and I can tell you this: it doesn't matter how much money you have, how many keys you have on your keychain or how big and powerful you think you are, **cancer is the great equalizer.** It doesn't give a damn about money, it doesn't give a damn about who you are or what you've done. When you get it, you're IT and if you're lucky, you get a jump on the disease. If you just bury your head in the sand, like many men do, then you're toast. And those men who thought they would never get tagged were the ones I wanted to reach.

PROSTATE CANCER RESEARCH INITIATIVE
Lester Smith, Chairman
Houston, Texas

051301

October 13, 2003 Date

to the *Baylor College of Medicine* $1,100,000
of _____

one million one hundred thousand and no/100 DOLLARS

Lester Smith

MEMO *Prostate Cancer Golf Tournament Proceeds*

At Baylor College of Medicine's annual golf tournament raising money for prostate cancer research.

Prostate cancer is the second leading cause of cancer death for men in the United States, after lung cancer, and the sixth leading cause of death for men overall, according to the Centers for Disease Control and Prevention. More than 70 percent of all diagnosed prostate cancers are found in men aged sixty-five years or older, but all men are at risk.

We presented the campaign to the very doctors at Baylor College of Medicine who had saved my life, and before anyone could stop the runaway train, we had the first of many events to raise funds and attention for the cause.

In March 2004 we received our first check for $5,000 from Encore Bank, presented by golf legend and prostate cancer survivor **Arnold Palmer.** It was a good start, but I knew we could raise more money.

Despite my utter disregard for research during my college years, I spent considerable time doing just that—looking at how other organizations raised money. There were many good approaches, but none really grabbed me. As an oil man, I thought we could put a business spin on raising awareness and funds for prostate cancer research. But there just didn't seem to be a good model in place, until I read about Mike Milken.

Regardless of what anyone thinks of Mike, he has faced his share of challenges—both in his professional and personal life—head on, even when he was diagnosed with prostate cancer in 1993. He was told he had **less than two years to live.** Imagine hearing that! Did he roll up into a ball and cry? Maybe he did. But Mike didn't

Arnold Palmer and me after receiving our first check on March 2, 2004, for prostate cancer research.

accept that prognosis. Instead, he went to work to change it. Single handedly, he raised the profile of prostate cancer by establishing the **Prostate Cancer Foundation,** giving and raising millions to fund promising research programs.

When I read about Mike, I decided I needed to meet him face to face. I thought maybe I could hustle him out of some money for Baylor's prostate cancer research program. Maury Abramson, Jan Carson and I flew out to Los Angeles ready to get our hustle going. We had all the materials we knew a smart guy like Mike Milken needed— lots of reports with numbers. Boy, were we wrong! I was so taken by his sincerity and his total devotion to finding a cure, I ended up writing *him* a check for the **Home Run Challenge.** Who got hustled? I did—and it was one of the best things I have ever done. And, get this—he also talked me into joining the Prostate Cancer Foundation board. Since then, Sue and I have enjoyed visiting him at his home in Lake Tahoe, and we consider him a good friend to this day.

In June 2004 Mike invited Sue and me to the Home Run Challenge, an event he established with Major League Baseball teams around the country. In select games played around **Father's Day,** each home run raises money for prostate cancer research. Since it was established in 1996, the Home Run Challenge has raised more than $25 million for prostate cancer research.

We had the pleasure of meeting baseball Hall of Famer Tommy Lasorda, who greeted us like we were old friends. What a tremendous honor it was to present a super-sized check from The Smith Foundation to the Prostate Cancer Foundation, celebrating our shared mission to fund research and find a cure. **Standing on home plate in Houston's Minute Maid Park** with our hometown team, the Astros, and hearing 58,000 fans roar was thrilling for me.

And it only got better. Toward the end of the *Honor Your Father Campaign*, Mike presented us a check for half a million dollars to fund prostate cancer research at Baylor College of Medicine. He was a class act. A few months later, Mike made the cover of *Fortune* magazine along with **Lance Armstrong,** one of many well-known people who jumped on the Mike Milken "Kick Cancer's Butt" bandwagon, working with him to find a cure. Imagine my great delight at seeing a photo of Sue and me with Mike and Tommy Lasorda included in the article. Prior to that my only connection to *Fortune* magazine had been seeing my name on a mailing label.

It was a great start to the campaign, but it was time to mobilize the troops. On September 9, 2004, the campaign leadership team was on the steps of **city hall with then-Mayor Bill White,** my good friend and neighbor. Cameras rolling, we announced Houston's first ever prostate cancer campaign to not only raise awareness and funds, but also to provide free PSA screenings all over town. Our buddies at HEB food stores were more than happy to help, as were literally hundreds of others, from volunteers to the medical community.

The Smith Foundation provided the funding to test more than 10,000 men for prostate cancer and along the way I know that we saved many hundreds of lives. I must commend Jan and her staff for making it all happen. I had the easy job really. All I had to do was talk (like that's hard for me) and spend some money (which I have been known to do).

And I talked so much about it, we decided it was time to take it to the airwaves. Because the number one thing that scared men to death was losing sexual function, we needed to set the record straight.

Jan put on her news-anchor hat once again and partnered with KTRK-TV, ABC/13 to present a half-hour special report we called **"Love, Sex & PSA."** It aired numerous times throughout the campaign and reached more than two million viewers. We were delighted when we learned that the special had won awards, including a Lone Star Emmy. Months later we were humbled to be recognized at the Association of Fundraising Professionals (AFP) international conference in Atlanta where General Colin Powell presented us with the AFP Excellence in Fundraising Award. It was a proud moment in my life.

But the moments that truly stand out from the campaign were the families I met. If I learned one thing, it was this: **a disease impacts everyone in the family.** That's why the name *Honor Your Father* was so spot on.

Men don't want to talk about prostate cancer, but I knew that if we could help break down the misconceptions, old wives' tales—or is that old husbands' tales?—and

It was absolutely thrilling to be with baseball legend Tommy Lasorda and Mike Milken at Minute Maid Park watching our much loved Houston Astros and presenting a check to the Home Run Challenge to support vital prostate cancer research.

fear, we could really change the future for many men and ultimately save some lives. We could mobilize men—fathers, husbands, sons—and the women who loved them to take an **active role in their health and get screened.** We could also increase understanding of prostate cancer, encourage early detection and focus on what Baylor College of Medicine does best—research aimed at a cure, with doctors to take it from the bench to the bedside.

Throughout the campaign, I met guys as young as twenty-eight and men much older than I was who had suffered from prostate cancer. And in addition to their diagnosis, they all shared another trait—they were willing to **share their own personal stories** to encourage other men. In short, they were brave. Because I can tell you, cancer is the scariest place on earth. But it's not so frightening when you can hold someone else's hand through it all.

While chairing Baylor's Prostate Cancer Research Initiative (PCRI), I spent hours each week at various initiatives (read that four syllable word as "meetings to discuss how much money they need." But my most wonderful experiences came from meeting and peer-counseling other men suffering from prostate cancer.

Immersed in the role of **patient advocate,** I was touched to hear so many personal stories. I knew without a doubt that our collective work was vital and essential. During that year, I was on the phone three to four hours every night trying to console a newly diagnosed patient and often speaking to his wife or another loved one as well.

208

Most of all, I sat silent, listening, listening, listening. This big talker realized that the best thing I could ever do was to be quiet and just listen to these people. Just "be" with them.

I counseled more than three hundred men the first year I headed up PCRI, and guess what? **I didn't lose one person.** Thank God. Because of all of that testing and a lot of help from above, we caught everyone early.

The big finale was next. As former competitive dancers, Sue and I had such fun planning the *Honor Your Father* Gala, "It Takes Two to Tango." With more than 1200 guests, we decided that we needed two ballrooms, three bands and one big checkbook. We hired **former U.S. champion ballroom dancers** to put on the floorshow, but also more than thirty professional ballroom dancers to get our guests moving and shaking on the dance floor. If you've never tangoed or cha-cha'ed with a really good dancer, go out and do it tonight. You'll fall in love, want to dance all night and be sore as hell in the morning. And you'll want to do it all over again tomorrow.

We had a live auction, a big board auction, and we would have auctioned off my toupee, *if* I wore one—anything to raise more money, because every dime was going to research. We had an unbelievable showcase of Latin dancers—you know the ones with the Chiquita Banana–looking headdresses that look as if they will topple over any second. But these dancers were pros. No toppling. We had **eye-popping floorshows** with pulsating lights, an incredible menu, fine wines and loads of professional photographers

It Takes Two to Tango Gala in May 2005. We raised a record-breaking $6.4 million for prostate cancer research at Baylor College of Medicine.

to make everyone feel like a star.

But the best part was the check presentation. I just love a big check presentation. But I really, really love a *big* check presentation *and* a big surprise. What I really hate is stopping the music and trying to get people to listen, but it didn't really matter. I figured we'd pose for a couple of photos for the college yearbook and get back to what we were doing—having a ball.

But as soon as the music stopped, all **eyes were on the stage** and you could hear a pin drop. Almost. We had a video camera set up in the second ballroom so no one missed the action. Even Baylor's president didn't know the final amount. Drum roll, please. There were a few gasps when we unveiled the check and revealed the final number. The campaign raised $6.4 million to fund prostate cancer research. It was the largest single fund-raiser in Baylor College of Medicine's history, and it wouldn't be topped until two years later when we raised a whopping $23 million for breast cancer research.

Now the applause was great and yada yada yada, I loved all the pats on the back, but what was really perfect was living up to one of my favorite mottos: **anything worth doing is worth overdoing.**

When the campaign began, the campaign committee set our fund-raising goal really high. I already knew from the very beginning that we'd have a pretty good chance of beating that number, but I didn't breathe a word to anyone. I wanted them working hard all the way through to the end. And working toward the goal of visualizing a bigger number and knowing how great it was going to be to hand that big check over and seeing the faces of all those physicians and survivors and husbands and wives so happy to know that we were doing something unprecedented for prostate cancer—well, it was glorious. Out of the blue, and as a total surprise to Sue and me, a new name was created, *The Lester and Sue Smith Urologic Clinic at Baylor College of Medicine*. I had neither asked for that nor expected it. My goal was beating prostate cancer, not having some clinic named after me. **There were loads of tears that night—all mine.**

So I say challenge yourself, reach for the stars and when it's appropriate—OVERDO. **Don't settle for vanilla.** Make it a double banana split with hot fudge, butterscotch, strawberries, chocolate chips, nuts, whipped cream and three cherries on top—the works! Sort of like the headdresses those dancers wore. And after that, go dancing with your sweetie. Do the hustle, the jive and the salsa. Thank the good Lord you are alive, and remember, it takes two to tango. And always remember what Lester Smith has to say: **don't ever give up, just keep trying and anything worth doing is worth overdoing.**

How joyous!

Sue and I had such fun chairing the Orange Show Gala in 2006.
It wasn't hard to figure out what color to wear.

12

real men wear pink

We were all gathered in Dr. Brunicardi's office with solemn faces; my children were pale-faced, **silent tears streaming down their cheeks.** Their mother, Barbara, had been diagnosed with metastatic breast cancer. And the prognosis at that time was grim.

The next few hours were a blur of running to different floors to consult with other physicians—and when I say running, we were running as if our lives depended on it. It was sheer panic, and we all felt desperate to do whatever we could to help her through that hellish day and figure out the best plan of action. Because that is the issue—when you get that diagnosis, you just don't know what to do.

We all thrive on having a plan, don't we? And it seems that throughout our lives, we are busy preparing for the various roles we will play on that big stage. We go to college to become math teachers, accountants, lawyers and doctors. But I don't remember signing up for the "Cancer for Dummies" course. I probably would have flunked it anyway. All of us would. That is one bad-ass course that we hope and pray isn't on our course schedule in the school of Life.

As a cancer survivor, I can tell you with complete certainty that you don't hear much of what the doctors are saying to you when you receive the shocking news. All you here is this, and it is like a bullhorn in your ears: **YOU HAVE CANCER.** And the only thing you want to know is: am I going to die?

And you know what? What you really, *really* want the good doc to say during that critical time when you learn of your diagnosis is this: **THERE IS HOPE.**

We want to believe that the mean buggar called cancer will hit the road, Jack. And as the song goes, "dontcha come back no more, no more, no more, no more."

It may be a surprise to you that Sue and I were right there, along with Barbara's husband, Bill. Despite the divorce, Barbara and I remain very close, and there is absolutely nothing I wouldn't do for her.

Barbara is such a wonderful person, a dedicated mother and grand-

Sue and I were joined by Andrea White at the 2004 Race for the Cure.

mother and she didn't deserve this, especially after all I put her through. During my diagnosis of bladder cancer she took such great care of me. We had fallen in love in our teens and were married for twenty-six years. During that time she was always **waiting for the day that I would quit working so hard.** That day is yet to come.

As a person of action, I knew the first order of business—she needed to see a first-rate team of physicians. If there is one thing I know how to do besides drilling oil wells, it's this: I am a matchmaker extraordinaire when it comes to **pairing patients with doctors,** and the best are right here in Houston at Baylor College of Medicine and MD Anderson Cancer Center. I knew with complete certainty that Barbara would be in the best hands.

This was not our first experience with a breast cancer diagnosis. It took Sue and me back through a whirlwind of emotions that we had felt surrounding the death of Sue's sister Pat, who succumbed to the ravages of the disease in 2000.

Like many men and women, Pat's diagnosis came too late, with little hope for a complete recovery. Still, she fought breast cancer for five long, painful years. Before our eyes, she was tortured to death. Her cancer was so horrific; there is no other way to describe it. And you know why it lasted so long? Every fiber of Pat's being was focused entirely on living for her children and grandchildren.

We were at her bedside when she died. I will always remember it because **I made a silent vow**—to do whatever I could to ensure that other women had better outcomes.

I cared for Pat, and I know Sue felt her loss very deeply, but I wasn't prepared for the anger Sue felt at her sister's death. Months, even years, later Sue has struggled with the frustration of **not being able to do more for her sister.**

"Pat was just a number, with little access to personalized care," she's told me more times than I can count. "No one deserves to be just another cancer patient. Everyone deserves to be treated with respect and dignity and provided with the best available treatment options."

Breast cancer is **deeply buried in my psyche.** After Pat died, and after Barbara's diagnosis, I knew that the course of my life would be marked by **supporting efforts to find a cure.**

In 2004 our foundation became a sponsor of the *Susan G. Komen Race for the Cure*, and Sue and I were invited to participate in the opening ceremony. We were there to not only support the race but to share information about our newly formed campaign to raise awareness and funding for prostate cancer research. What better place **to encourage men to get tested** than an event with tens of thousands of women? And guess why? It's the women who do the nudging. It works every time.

It was *very* early in the morning, and Sue and I got up to the podium to speak just before **the race was to begin.** As I gazed at the crowd of more than 27,000, I was literally speechless. There were young women, older women, women of every color and size. There were women bearing the marks of their cancer with headscarves or showing

*It was a very humbling experience to be at the 2004 Race for the Cure and look out
at a crowd of over 27,000 people gathered to fight breast cancer.*

off a bald head, some with peach fuzz just starting to grow back. There were men too. It was an ocean of people who had gotten out of bed on a very early Saturday morning in October to run or walk for a cure for a disease that strikes one in eight women. Some runners wore signs on their backs bearing the names of survivors. Too many children wore signs in memory of their mothers and grandmothers who had lost their battle with the disease. **I was so choked up,** I could hardly speak.

Following the race, we manned a booth, and Pat's children were there to help. It was humbling for me to see and meet so many people who were dedicated to finding a cure. Because when you've got it, **you really do GET IT,** if you know what I mean.

Cancer survivors look at life very differently from those who have not battled the disease. Cancer is truly a battle on all fronts—physical, spiritual and emotional. Each of us bears the war wounds differently, and it is from this struggle that we find in ourselves a reason to go on. We are forever changed by this experience. Having cancer prompts us to take action in ways that we might never otherwise consider.

I can tell you this—**I never considered giving away so much** until cancer impacted me and my loved ones personally. I made a promise, not unlike the one Nancy Brinker, Komen's founder, made to her dying sister, to do something. And if you are going to do something, **do it big,** I always say. I would dedicate my resources to finding a cure and caring for those who battle the disease. Sue and I believed it was especially important to provide access to quality care for those who—like Pat—were just numbers.

221

That promise was realized in 2007, when Sue and I were at a press conference announcing The Smith Foundation's major grant to Baylor College of Medicine. Baylor was so happy, they named the Breast Center for us. Now that was a big surprise! After much thought, discussions with Dr. Kent Osborne and Dr. Richard Gibbs, tours and meetings with researchers at the bench and lots of homework on our own, we decided to earmark funds for both breast cancer research and genomic medicine. We learned then and still strongly believe that the delivery of personalized medicine is linked to advances made in genomic research. And we are lucky enough to have one of the leading breast cancer and genomic research centers in the world right in our own backyard.

It is hard to understand how important that access is until **you or a loved one is struck by a disease.** My cowboy hat goes off to the men and women who work around the clock, hunched over a computer or in a lab, working to find that missing link to a cure.

There is a wonderful program on National Public Radio called "The Long View." Listen to it sometime. I recently heard Rabbi Harold Kushner, who wrote the famous book *When Bad Things Happen to Good People*. When I was diagnosed with cancer, I kept asking that universal question: **"Why me, God?"**

We want to know the reason we are sick. Was it because I was a bad person? Because I had lied in Hebrew school about missing class (I was back behind the gym with a

I never considered giving **away so much until cancer** impacted me and my loved ones personally.

pack of Camels) or because at times in my life I drank too much? And if I deserved this punishment, my family certainly did not. They were along for the ride-from-hell, too. It didn't seem fair. And it certainly doesn't seem fair that too many mothers, wives, sisters, daughters, grandmothers and loved ones get struck with breast cancer.

In Kushner's new book, *Overcoming Life's Disappointments*, he writes about looking back on our lives and reflecting on goals we made that were never fully realized. He says we have to **let go of the notion** that we somehow failed at doing what we set out to do.

And you know what? He's right. Each of us has some kind of benchmark formed early in our lives, and reaching it would mean that we had achieved our heart's desires and achieved success. I'm all about goal-setting and realizing dreams, but I have also learned in my own long view at age sixty eight, that sometimes **we have to rethink our notion of success.** More often than not, a diagnosis of cancer—or other health or economic challenges—becomes a detour off the super-highway of life we're on and seems to put the brakes on what we ever hoped to achieve. Remember this— health may not be everything, but if you lose it, everything soon becomes nothing. And all the great success in the world doesn't matter much if you are not around to enjoy it.

That thought was made crystal clear to me when Sue and I attended the recent funeral of our good friend, the late Dan Duncan. Dan and his sweet wife, Jan, lived

Dan Duncan and his lovely wife, Jan, at the 2010 Komen Pink Tie Gala. I miss my dear friend very much.

their lives with the end in sight. In short, Dan **lived like he was dying**, as the country song goes, and Jan continues to embrace life with the same passion. The last time we saw Dan was at Komen's Pink Tie Gala just a few weeks before he passed away unexpectedly. And there he was, dressed perfectly for the occasion.

"What a great pink tie," I said, noting his nod to the gala's theme and mission. "You know what they say, 'real men wear pink,'" I said, giving him a hug.

"I've missed you, Lester," Dan said.

"I've missed you too," I replied.

Dan's death is a reminder that **life is fragile.** His life is a reminder that success comes in many forms—and most of it has very little to do with money.

Today **my idea of success** is not about accumulating more stuff. It is much more **about encouraging others to succeed,** especially when it comes to alleviating human suffering. Nothing gives me more pleasure than knowing my time, talent and treasure can help someone far smarter than I will ever be find a cure for cancer or other deadly diseases. But it doesn't stop there. To fully realize that expertise, we must ensure that patients have access to it and benefit from it. Nothing is more rewarding than knowing that my gifts will help someone struggling with cancer to find hope again.

So join me as we **race, walk, swing, strut and dance to find a cure.** Volunteer to be an advocate for those suffering with the disease and contribute to those whose efforts are saving lives. If you are a survivor, share your hope-filled message with others. And while their battle scars may not be as visible, caregivers need our support, too. Take the time to hear their stories, share a hug or laugh, and yes, even tears. Remember, **big boys do cry, and real men wear pink.** Take it from me.

226

Remember, big boys do cry, and real men wear pink. Take it from me.

[13]

if these walls could talk

One of **our biggest joys** is opening up our home to family and friends. We built such a large home for exactly this reason. I cannot describe how much enjoyment we get out of the sounds of the house bustling with people, not to mention the din when the grandchildren arrive, running down the stairs, squealing in delight through the hallways. Those **precious children** make our home come alive with their laughter; they are such a joy to Sue and me.

We have hosted thousands of people in our home at a variety of events from family brunches, Passover seders and even—we are so pleased to say—a bris for our only grandson. We've had underwriter parties, fund-raisers, membership drives, and professional dance floorshows featuring some of the world's most celebrated ballroom dancers. We've waltzed, cha-cha'ed and rumba'ed under a **psychedelic rotating disco ball** until the wee hours. Outside of family functions, these events are opportunities for us to open our home to help many non-profit organizations with their outreach efforts and to build a sense of community.

Because, in the end, it is that **sense of community** that truly keeps us writing those checks, and attending those luncheons, galas and lectures. Or in our case, throwing a few parties.

And all in the name of raising awareness and of course cash for non-profit organizations not only here in Houston but around the world, we have indeed thrown a few.

One week, we hosted two back-to-back champagne luncheons, and we invited hundreds of people in an effort to help one of **our favorite charities** increase their membership. I might add that it worked: membership in the Baylor College of Medicine Partnership is currently at an all-time high, increasing over 500 percent. We've welcomed presidents and first ladies, dignitaries from around the world, authors, actors, entertainers, ballerinas, opera stars, singers and world-renowned physicians. We have

We've welcomed presidents and first ladies, dignitaries from around the world, authors, actors, entertainers, ballerinas, opera stars, singers and world-renowned physicians.

Sue, Trish Morille and Lisa Holthouse hamming it up with The Village People at the 2007 Baylor Gala.

also offered our guest room to cancer patients visiting one of Houston's outstanding treatment centers.

Over the years, I have watched in awe as Sue has joined me in welcoming each of these guests with not only an open hand, but more importantly, **an open heart.** Sue could teach the United Nations a thing or two about diplomacy, especially because she often has to think on her feet. And I mean that literally.

Take the time Sir Bob Geldof was in our home. Perhaps best known of late as one of the world's leading humanitarians, Sir Bob was in town to receive the Holocaust Museum Houston's Lyndon Baines Johnson Moral Courage Award.

Sue and I always **greet each guest at the door.** This custom can prove to be quite a feat, as sometimes the guest list numbers begin with two or three and end in several zeros. Cool as a cucumber, Sue never seems rattled. She looks each guest in the eye, takes both hands in hers, gives her trademark dazzling smile and always has a warm remark to put each visitor at ease. I have learned so much from her.

But enough about her.

We'd been told in advance that Sir Bob would not stay more than a few minutes. We were glad that he had finally arrived so we could move to the ballroom—it's my favorite place. No postage stamp–sized ballroom there. Because of our devotion to the art of dance, we had it built to ballroom standard specifications.

Sir Bob was absolutely charming, and he seemed totally taken with Sue. But she seemed pretty smitten with him too. Let's face it, **women absolutely swoon** over a man with an accent. No, not my East Texas twang that combines nails and a chalkboard in a merry union. This guy could tell you to go to hell, and you'd ask for directions just to hear him talk a bit more. If his voice wasn't enough, he's also a former rock star, for God's sake. And did I mention the hair? There he was: tall, handsome, a full head of hair, Irish, speaking with that wonderful accent and holding hands with my beautiful wife. And there I was: all alone, short, bald, big nose, feeling like a hick with an "aw' shucks" accent. I was clearly outmatched 10-to-1. But I still had a trick or two up my sleeve. I knew I could **one-up him on the dance floor.** Just wait, buddy!

Still standing at the door, I made a formal welcome to our guests. I had just turned to introduce Sir Bob, when he **grabbed my bride** by the hand and—having learned of our dancing abilities—proceeded to spin her around and dip her backwards in her three-inch heels! **Sue never lost a beat.** Years of dance training and yoga took over, and she made it look completely planned and effortless. On the other hand, I was about to let him have it. Imagine the nerve! He did it all wrong! You never spin your partner from the left, only the right. For God's sake, Sir Bob, you drive on the left in England, we drive on the right over here. If this was "American Idol," I was Simon, and I was about to give him the boot. My boot was ready, too. He would have gotten a **nice pointy toe** right in the ole bum.

"Good evening," I said loudly to the crowd gathered at the door. "I'm quite sure you

Sir Bob Geldof was smitten with my wife. Who came blame him?
Of course, she falls for those English accents every time.

know that our honored guest, Sir Bob Geldof, has twirled in."

"Sir Bob," I continued, looking at him straight in the eye. "This isn't the UK. This is Texas, son. And in Texas, when you grab another's man's wife, you'd better **grab your hat** and run!" My goodness, I didn't expect him to bend over with such a big belly laugh. So much for my machismo!

Of course, it was all in good fun. And it seemed that Sir Bob's other commitments that evening could wait. Despite his handlers reminding us repeatedly that he would only stay a few minutes, he stayed for well over an hour. As I recall, he showed his own **finesse on the dance floor** more than once. But who was counting? I was, of course! Wouldn't you know the rascal was a terrific dancer? And his tango—oh my! And—yes, it's about her again—he only had eyes for Sue. Who can blame him?

Another big moment occurred in our ballroom in 2009. We had the privilege of having Madeleine Albright in our home, and I have to admit that I was in awe. Not only was she the first female secretary of state, I had heard she was a really terrific dancer. I know, I know. I'm completely shallow. It's not that I wasn't interested in how she expanded or modernized NATO, promoted peace in the Balkans or got in the face of China on their human rights record. All that is good, really good. **But could she dance?** I was determined to find out.

I had to pick my moment.

First of all, I had timing to consider. Due to one of Houston's famed tropical storm-turned-hurricane episodes, the original event had been canceled and the new date gave us very little wiggle room. This event was to be an hour-long reception, prior to a free public lecture our foundation presents with the Holocaust Museum Houston—The Lester and Sue Smith Distinguished Lecture Series. The lecture was to take place across town at Houston Baptist University to a crowd of over 1500. We had barely one hour. I felt like Tom Cruise in *Mission Impossible*. **The bald version.**

After being alerted that she was to arrive within minutes, we gathered the two hundred or so people around the foyer and waited. I was a nervous wreck. Necks craned to see her, and with her usual briskness, she came through the door and greeted us warmly by name. What a pro. First of all, she is tiny. But don't kid yourself. This is a woman who helped reduce Russia's nuclear threat to the free world! And she has all those letters and dots after her name. I admit that, on occasion, I do have "initial" envy.

Well, **Mr. Mouth made another appearance,** and remarked, "Well, I have finally met someone shorter than me!" Not under my breath or anything, but out loud for the entire world to hear. Everyone had a great laugh over that one, including Madam Secretary, thank the good Lord.

Sue came to my rescue. She was completely unflappable. It is one of the things I adore about her. She will greet both a former secretary of state and the mailman with the same **gracious warmth.** And she means it with all her heart.

We escorted Madam Secretary around to meet members of the museum's board, introduced her to other guests and watched as she patiently spoke to each guest who greeted her with keen interest. After a long series of posed photographs, which she endured with complete composure, I had my moment. But she took the words right out of my mouth.

"I've heard that you and Sue are excellent dancers," she said. **"May I see the ballroom?"**

Music to my ears! We whisked her upstairs with only minutes to spare. Just the three of us, followed by her assistant.

"Oh my," she breathed. "What a beautiful ballroom!" I could tell she was impressed. It is a pretty ballroom, I must admit.

When Sue and I got married, we took a few dance lessons in preparation for our wedding and honeymoon in Vienna. I just wanted to learn how to waltz so I wouldn't look like a complete idiot in our wedding video. But after learning the waltz, we wanted **more . . . and more and more.** Yes, there is a pattern here. Within a few years, we were spending four hours a day with private coaches here and abroad, touring for weeks and competing around the United States. In 2002 and 2003 we won two titles in the U.S. Grand Senior Latin Champions. Hence, the ballroom.

It was designed with a custom sound and light system and the **ubiquitous disco ball** in the ceiling; you know, the norm.

Former Secretary of State Madeleine Albright in our home in 2009. Who knew she was also such a great dancer?

With a quick press of a button, the sound of my theme song, "I Will Survive," began to pulsate in the room, lights flashing to the beat. I took Sue's hand and we "hustled" our way across the floor. It's just about the best dance song ever written.

What happened next, I would never have expected.

"Dance with me, Lester!" the former secretary of state commanded. I could see how she was confirmed unanimously by the United States Senate. She was a **tiny force to be reckoned with.**

I was more than happy to oblige. I actually adore taking orders from powerful women; at least that's what my therapist says.

I took her tiny hand in mine and, in an effort to impress her, made the rounds of every dance step I knew, starting with my favorite—**the hustle.** What a great dancer she was! She didn't miss a beat. It was almost just like dancing with Sue, only this was the former U.S. secretary of state! What a thrill for me. For the record, it was not as thrilling as dancing with my wife, but still . . . great fun!

I spun her around in a number called the **Spanish Arms** where the partners end up in a dramatic "nose to nose" finish. I pulled her straight into my face and she giggled. Yes, she really giggled. There I was, nose to nose with Madam Secretary. It was a fantastic moment and one I will treasure; I hope she feels the same way.

After the dance, I told her about some of the many parties we had hosted, including the most recent, Bikers, Babes & Blues party. She said she wanted to be invited to the next one.

"That would be wonderful," I answered. "But you might have to wear **black leather and a fake tattoo."**

"I can do that," she answered. And I bet she can.

What a pro and a lady! I looked over at Sue. She was smiling broadly as she applauded.

A thoughtful note followed barely one week later, "Thank you for your generous hospitality."

I would like to think I have a little to do with our hospitality, but in fact, that is really not all about me; rather, it is all about the warmth, generosity and total class of my dear wife. Over the last fourteen years, not only has Sue taught me to say the word "gracious" without tripping over my tongue, she has in fact been **my greatest mentor** when it comes to helping people feel immediately at ease, a feat few can truly pull off.

And I think it is because Sue knows what **true hospitality** means. It has more to do with how guests feel than how spotless the floors are.

Here's what hospitality is not about: lavish surroundings, exquisite food and beverage, the perfect pillow. It's about a real warmth and generosity of spirit that places true value where it should lie—in the dignity of a human being.

The Torah, the Bible and many other religious texts refer to hospitality as a **moral imperative.** Growing up in a small Jewish community, we were linked to one another through the practice of our faith but more importantly, through our shared experiences. These milestones of life provided my family with many opportunities to open our home sometimes to total strangers and instilled in me a desire to share what I have with others.

You know why? **It's the right thing to do.**

Much is expected of those who have much. I read that somewhere, and I think it's true. So **what do you have to share?** What can you do help end hunger, fight illiteracy, stop domestic violence or find a cure for breast cancer? Whatever your cause, pursue it, support it, nurture it and watch it grow. Open your heart—and if you can, your home too—and you'll find the **joy and warmth of giving** lingers long after the last guest says "good night."

242

Open your heart—
and if you can, your home too—
and you'll find the joy and warmth of giving

lingers long after the last guest says "good night."

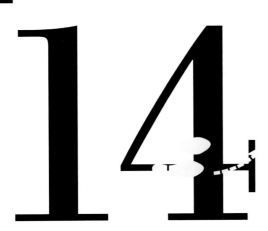14

the meaning of bald

I like being bald.

I wouldn't recommend it if you have a nice full head of hair—and I once did. I think I was twelve, or maybe thirteen. But it is one of those life-changing moments when you finally make the decision to **go naked up top.**

I decided to become bald when my hair was thinning and gray. But there were other **compelling reasons too.** When I was diagnosed with bladder cancer, the chemotherapy was contained inside my bladder.

To tell you the truth, the only place I had a fear of losing hair was, to put it delicately, not for public display. And as so many of my experiences with cancer seemed to do, it scared me to death. So with this big fear, and of course **the mother of all fears—dying—**and all my other real and imagined fears, my hair continued to get grayer and grayer and thinner and thinner. And there was absolutely nothing I could do about it. Or so I thought.

The decision to finally reveal the full extent of my shiny noggin was rooted in finally accepting this fact. It was also rooted in a much more serious desire: **I wanted to be sexy.**

C'mon, you know it's true! Women find bald-headed men irresistible. Think about the late Yul Brynner, Bruce Willis or the late Telly Savalas, whose famous quip, "Who Loves Ya Baby?" would never sound as provocative if he'd been wearing a rug. In fact, he's also quoted as saying, **"We're all born bald."** Love ya, man. Mean it.

Women love bald men for loads of reasons. There's no one fighting them for mousse, hairspray, gel or the shower cap. You never have to worry about going gray again. Life is simpler, yet more exotic. It takes a pretty confident man to clear the cranium, so to speak. And—get this—I read that male pattern baldness can be caused by an excess of testosterone. We all know what that could mean. **Think about it.**

So I decided that if my cancer treatment was going to make me feel like crap and, one way or another, force me to lose what was left of my hair, I needed a jump on the

Look at that bald headed guy with the hot mama. We were sure in love then and we still are today.

The Paso Doble, "The Bull Fight Dance," is one serious dance. It is either you or the bull.

"sexy meter." Going bald was it.

Men have a hard time with this. Believe me, I know. You know these guys, too. There's the infamous "comb-over" type. You know, the poor man who just won't admit that he's balding so he combs his hair forward, starting at the base of his neck. The three-strand comb-overs are the absolute worst. The poor schmuck has three hairs left and God help him, he is not parting with them. Those strands are a lifeline to his full-head-of-hair past, and he clings to them like a lucky charm. Hey, buddy, just shave it off, get an earring and wear some spandex like the rest of us men. Men dancers, that is.

Then there's the "rug man," the guy who is too embarrassed to show his shrinking hairline, choosing instead to cover it with some cheap imitation. Like no one knows! Andre Agassi says that **wearing a toupee** was one of the reasons he lost the French Open in 1990. In his book he says he was so worried his rug would fall off, he couldn't focus on his game. And those hair pins sticking out for the entire world to see were probably not good for his concentration either.

I spoke to Sue about it. She was all for a smooth dome.

"And if you don't like it, it'll grow back," she noted. **Now that was thinking positively!**

So I got in the shower, lathered up my head and went to work shaving it. There wasn't much to shave, but it was a great feeling to go through the motions.

Going bald took some getting used to. I had to learn to be careful not to burn my head, so **sunscreen became a daily habit.** I got colder too. And everyone wants to touch it, like some Buddhist ritual. When they start rubbing my belly, it's over.

But what really surprised me was how other people reacted to it.

I think going bald actually helped Sue and me as competitive dancers on more than one occasion. First of all, the judges could remember the bald guy with the strikingly gorgeous partner. And it gave us an edgy look as Latin dancers. I added an earring, and wow, did that make a big impression. Watch out, Montel.

The earring became my bald head's best friend. And of course, the attention it provided **fed my soul like mother's milk.** I was lovin' it!

Five weeks after my prostate cancer surgery, I was back on the dance floor getting ready for a big competition when I realized I was late for a doctor's appointment. I literally jumped in the car and headed to the Scott Department of Urology without a second glance.

Dr. Seth Lerner, a consummate professional and outstanding physician, was giving me the once over when I noticed that he kept staring slightly right of my line of vision. I checked my shoulder. No spider or dandruff there. **Certainly no lost hairs!** Something on the wall behind me? Negative. Then I got it. **He was staring at my earring.**

"Dr. Lerner, are you staring at my earring?" I asked.

This is one of my all-time favorite photos, taken at the Ohio Star Ball as we were dancing the samba.

"Uh, no," he mumbled. He was busted. I knew it and he knew it. He finally looked directly at me, rather sheepishly.

"Okay, Lester, I admit it. I was staring at your earring."

He was envious. Most men are. It takes a lot of balls to be bald and wear an earring. Especially at age fifty-nine!

After I told him where he could get some nice diamond studs like mine for his wife, he was happy. And I was happy, because if there is anything I love to do, it is to shake things up a bit. This little episode gave me the courage to start wearing my earring nearly 24/7.

I wore the diamond stud to galas and business meetings. I think there was more than one meeting at the Petroleum Club about it. Thank goodness they did not kick me out. I made sure to pay my dues on time. And I had a little gold hoop I would wear out to dinner or to the movies. Then I'd forget about it for awhile, the hole would close up and I'd have to take a needle and stick myself again.

But it was all worth it—a good laugh or two, or three, with some shock value thrown in for good measure. And what's more, it leveled the playing field a time or two. The **"bald guy with the earring"** look brought me into contact with some pretty interesting people and made me perhaps more approachable. I like that.

But the word "bald" also conjured up a lot of emotion for people who, like me, had struggled with cancer. Some well-intentioned people actually thought that my decision to go bald was because of my cancer. **And indirectly, it was.**

I hadn't lost all my hair due to chemotherapy, but what going bald meant for me was definitely about letting go. Letting go, doing something daring and saying to the world, "There's more to me than meets the eye."

And those were the exact words I used when I received a call from a friend late one night. My friend Alan, in his sixties, was newly retired from a successful business, with plans to travel the world with his wife of forty years. Just a few weeks into retirement, he learned he had cancer. And it didn't look good.

He asked me what he should do.

"That's easy," I answered. "First, get into bed, curl up in a ball and have a really good cry," I suggested. I could tell that he wasn't expecting that answer. But when we can give ourselves permission to grieve—**even if we're big, ole tough oil guys**—we can then move on to making sense of our situation and eventually move toward hope. There are many more steps in this process, believe me. This is the Cliff's Notes version.

I kept in touch with Alan during his treatment, his chemotherapy and his radiation. I even talked to his wife several times. She told me that his hair was falling out in big clumps and he was too embarrassed to leave the house. Poor guy. He must have missed that "Today Show" segment: **"Bald: Is it Hot or Not?" It was definitely hot.**

I told Alan that there were many things he couldn't control—his cancer being first and foremost on that list. But he could control his hair loss. He was probably thinking I could recommend a good "plug" doctor, but instead I told him to let it go. **Go for it. Go bald.**

Just the idea that someone in the grips of cancer, fighting for his or her life, *can* control something is a huge step in finding hope. And in my friend's case—it was just that. Learning to let go is such a huge step—and it's not about giving up. NO! It's about **having realistic expectations and making good choices** that foster our own growth and well-being. Maybe not our hair growth, but you get the idea.

254

You know what else? I was proud that I could add to the Bald or Not debate by recruiting one more sexy guy to our ranks. I just might send him an earring.

dwelling with my star

Sue and I are known as The Dancers. I love to brag about this because it almost killed us—just kidding, but it nearly did break up our marriage. Seriously, it was just about the hardest thing we have ever done in our twenty years together.

We were competitive ballroom dancers for eight and a half years from 1995 to 2003. When I say competitive, **I mean hard-core competitors.** To dance well and win was the highest of highs. I just love getting high, especially those super-duper natural highs. Add an adrenaline rush, and I'm off to the races.

We practiced with our coaches, teachers, choreographers and each other every day for four hours. For Sue,it was only three hours because she was much better than I was. That still makes me so mad.

"Look at Sue, how beautiful she looks on the floor."

"Sue is so elegant, she is so graceful, she is so poised, she looks just like a ballerina."

Sue this, Sue that! I wanted to ring her beautiful, elegant neck!

Now you can see the ugly truth. Dancing is tough on a marriage.

We practiced hard five days a week, year in and year out for over eight years. We were on the road forty to fifty days per year, entering ten to twelve competitions per year. Talk about hard work. OMG, we were sore all of the time. If we didn't do our thirty-minute stretching routine before we went to bed, when we woke up it was as if a train had run over us. Where were our crutches? We bought Advil™ by the case.

When you dance at such high competitive levels and are sore all the time, tempers run short. We had some really first-class arguments and screaming matches.

"You pulled me"; "You pushed me"; "You stepped on my foot" or the best one yet, **"You breathed at the wrong time and knocked my balance off."**

That would be during the rumba when we had tight body-to-body poses. I love the rumba, the dance of love. After every rumba practice I would say to Sue, "Let's go home right now. As I have something important I need to talk to you about in the bedroom."

258

I have wonderful rumba memories—those short skirts, the smell of perfume and our bodies super-glued together. **Rumba was one of our best dances.** I just love carrots and rumba was sure one big carrot to me. And Sue just adored the rumba, too. And was she good at it? Smokin'!

Yes, it was tough, but we also had loads of fun and met amazing people. We became members of an exciting sub-cult. And guess what? I got to wear my earring—no make that two—one gold loop and one diamond stud in my left ear. I wore those earrings 24/7 like they were some sacred military honor. **Talk about stares** from the business community.

We traveled all over the United State and trained in Europe, all for the love of dance and the rewards that came with it—ribbons, medals and the coveted first place trophies. Those were some very expensive doodads. We had an entourage, teachers and coaches, and then there were travel expenses and the fabulous costumes. **Neiman Marcus move over.**

We were rock stars (in our own minds), except we paid instead of getting paid. Something doesn't make sense here. Sure, it wasn't a good business deal, but it was fun. And it served us very well when we started raising money for charity. We really know how to throw a gala with all the glitz and glitter. All of our theatrical training has been put to great use, raising millions for charity. Talk about the floorshows and entertainment. Wow!

Our wedding in 1995 was one of the happiest days of my life. I'm so grateful she said "yes"!

Okay, I promised you I would brag. We danced in the over-age-fifty category. **Here comes the bragging part:** we were two-time United States Grand Senior Champions in International Latin, which is five different dances: cha-cha, samba, rumba, Paso Doble and jive. Our name is forever in the record books.

We worked so hard to be The Dancers. And it changed us. There are several ways I knew I had become a Dancer, not just a bald guy who danced.

You Know You Are A Dancer When:

- The price of a costume is the same as your monthly mortgage payment.

- You argue over who gets to wear the big diamond earrings . . . and you're the guy.

- Everyone wears tons of makeup. Not to mention the girls! Even the guys are confused for streetwalkers.

- You think pierced navels are good for both sexes.

- Your partner's costumes boast a half-yard of see-through material, tied together with a few strings and twenty-five pounds of rhinestones.

- Your hair gives new meaning to the phrase "helmet hair." Hurricane-force winds are no match for that case of styling gel. Unless you are bald.

- You wonder if there is any other color on earth besides black.

- You wonder why you can't make dinner reservations at 1:00 A.M.

- You ask your partner, "Do you think these six gold chains are enough around my neck?" And your partner answers, "Why so understated? Add more!"

- You wear so much self-tanner that people speak to you in Spanish first on every airline flight you take.

- You try to button your shirt, then you realize, **you have no buttons—or shirt.**

- If you have a shirt, you leave it unbuttoned so that everyone can see how well you coordinated your navel stud with the one in your ear.

- All that practice and dancing means you and your lady have two smokin' hot bods.

Now where did the dance drive come from? Let's talk about the genesis of this addiction.

My parents loved to have people over to our house in Wharton. My brothers and I grew up in a family that truly enjoyed being together and could take any occasion and make it a spirited social event. The best parties were the ones that required moving furniture around. **That meant we were going to dance!** Watching my parents and a long line of relatives and friends jitterbug and waltz were some of the happiest memories I have.

I took tap dancing lessons when I was four years old. At my first recital, I danced to "Camptown Races," wearing a blue and white satin jockey suit. Everyone was there—my parents, grandparents, the aunts and uncles. We were short on entertainment, I guess! I'll never forget the thrill of performing and hearing the crowd applaud wildly at the conclusion of the show. That night Lester the entertainer, sometimes known as Lester

We consistently placed first in our best two dances, the Paso Doble and the Jive, two of the five dances that comprise the International Latin.

Dancing the Paso Doble with my sweetie at the
2003 United States National Championship. Perfection!

the show-off, was born!

At age six I started playing the clarinet. I always played first or second chair. In high school I formed a band called the Bee Bops—trombone, sax, drums and clarinet. We had a big-band sound. We emulated Benny Goodman and Glenn Miller and **even had matching black satin jackets** with big birds on the back. Still, there was nothing that I loved more than dancing, even into adulthood.

Now the oil business and dancing are sort of like oil and water, pardon the pun. You don't generally think of the two in the same context, so I kept my dance longings under lock and key for many, many years. But the first time I danced with Sue, I realized it was time to ramp it up a bit. **After that first dance** I fell head over heels in love with her. I had been dancing since I was boy, but Sue was new to the ballroom floor—and she was a total natural. She had never taken dance lessons; in fact, as a teenager she was not allowed to go to dances. But she had a natural grace and ability on the dance floor that was **nothing short of astounding.** Getting to hold on to a gorgeous woman like her, and getting a little exercise too, seemed like a good way to spend my time away from the oil fields, too!

In 1995 when we started taking dance lessons, our dance instructor told us about a dance competition in San Antonio, and just for fun, we went to watch our new friends compete and to see what it was all about. We went not to dance but to be part of the cheering section. I remember seeing dozens of dancers all decked out in their incredible costumes, embellished with rhinestones and feathers. **They were so graceful, poised and beautiful.** Sue and I were enthralled with the glitz, glitter and physical demands of what is known as dance sport, and there was absolutely no question that we wanted to give competitive dancing a shot. And give it a shot is a major understatement: **we threw ourselves into the sport body and soul.**

In 1995 we spent our honeymoon in Vienna and went to the New Year's Eve Ball at the Winter Palace to dance none other than the **Viennese waltz, which was our very best dance.** It was nothing short of magical and I will never forget it. Around one in the morning, we decided to stir things up a bit, so we jumped on the stage and started to tango! We did a pretty mean tango, and oh, did we have fun that night.

We went back to Vienna and the Winter Palace in 2000 for the New Year's Eve Ball celebrating the millennium. We wanted to take another spin on that incredible dance floor. Rumor had it that royalty would be attending that evening. Sue was wearing a **gorgeous red velvet gown**. My sweetheart from West Virginia looked like royalty. It was like out of a movie set, and Sue was the star, the center of attention. **All eyes were on her.** We were dancing the Viennese waltz, making those grand sweeping turns that are the norm here in the United States. Austrians are known for their tight French turns. And there we were making these glorious turns, and the other couples were moving aside, motioning us to the center of the room, and before we knew it, the dance was over and the room broke into applause. A gentleman came over and

Here I am with the "Baroness" dancing at the
Winter Palace in Vienna on our honeymoom in 1995.

said, "Beautiful dancing, Baroness."

Sue looked at him and laughed, "I'm not a baroness, I'm Sue Smith from West Virginia, and we live in Texas!" You should have seen the look on his face. We all had a great laugh. Well, she certainly **looked like a baroness and sounded like a southern belle!**

Everyone wanted to dance with the "Baroness," and all night long I had to share her with a long line of men. Who could blame them for being totally smitten with her? It was a delight for me to see all those men act like a bunch of silly boys dancing with their first love.

"Hey boys, she belongs to me and when the party is over, we are going back to the hotel room, because we have something very, very important to talk about. Twice. Eat your hearts out." **Lucky me!**

It was New Year's Day and along the Shonbrunner Schloss Strasse were rows and rows of vendors selling spiced nuts and hot wine punch. Small groups of musicians were playing beautiful classical music, and we danced along one side of the street and back down the other side, with a light snow falling. We were dancers in our own little snow globe! It was like a page from a fairy tale and we were living it.

From 1995 to 2003 **we danced hard,** competing in the Grand Senior Division— for dancers over fifty—all over the world. We had dance instructors on two continents, and found ourselves dancing competitively in Houston, Dallas, San Antonio, San Francisco,

Los Angeles, Las Vegas, Atlanta, Columbus, Miami, Minneapolis-St Paul, Washington D.C. and Boston, among others. We also trained under the seventeen-time world champion, Donnie Burns, and another great champion Shirley Ballas.

Sue and I became proficient in **fourteen different dances,** including the International Latin, which includes the cha-cha, samba, rumba, Paso Doble, and jive. We have also competed and won competitions for the International Standard—the waltz, tango, Viennese waltz, foxtrot and quick step. And we love to dance the hustle, mambo, East Coast swing and West Coast swing on a social basis.

Dance became such a huge part of our lives, and we met so many talented young dancers that Sue and I decided to sponsor several of them. I will never forget seeing a very young Julianne Hough and her brother, Derek, or another hugely successful dancer, Mark Ballas, dance for the first time. Today when I see them winning on **"Dancing with the Stars,"** and getting music contracts and hit records, I feel so proud that I could help them in a very small way. Mark's mother, Shirley Ballas, was the center of all this. Regarded as one of the world's best Latin and ballroom dance instructors, she attained success winning numerous national and international titles. We were **lucky to have her as our main coach** for many years. She encouraged—or yelled, as the case may be—us to go for the gold, the United States Latin Championships. Little did I know that my dance career would be sidelined by a diagnosis of cancer.

In preparation for the National Championship, Sue and I traveled to Atlanta in

October 2001. I had just been diagnosed with aggressive prostate cancer, and it had spread outside of my prostate. Since I thought I was going to die, all I could do was roll up in a ball and cry. I certainly couldn't dance. I was watching Sue dance the Viennese waltz with her instructor, and it was all I could do to sit there without screaming my anguish out loud. Big tears rolled down my face **as I watched her dance** wondering if I would ever, ever dance with her again. Sue and her partner won the competition, and as they took their bows, she blew me a kiss. **It was the lowest point in my life.**

Back in Houston in November, I had my surgery and I was told it would be a good six months before I could dance again. I might add that they got all of the cancer and threw it in the trash can. I was good to go and that awful threat of death was gone. Over, kaput, finished and gone, and I was ready to go, healthy and "strong like russian bull." After a two-week stay in the hospital and three weeks of recuperation at home, I was back on the dance floor. If anything, my cancer diagnosis spurred me on to crank up the heat and go for the gold. And what did it take? Practice, practice and more practice!

Practice may not lead to perfection, but in our case, it did lead to winning some pretty big and exciting competitions. The highlight was in Provo, Utah, for the 2002 National Championship. It was held in the stadium at Brigham Young University. More than 10,000 people watched us perform the International Latin, our well-practiced, coached, choreographed and well-greased five-dance routine.

When the music ended after each dance, the crowd went wild! We bowed and waved

I was watching Sue dance the Viennese waltz with her instructor, and it was all I could do to sit there without screaming my anguish out loud.

our hands, palms up asking for more clapping and foot stomping. The crowd rose to their feet and gave us a standing ovation. We ate it up. Of course it really shook up the rest of the competitors. I was like Mick Jagger, strutting around the dance floor like a barnyard rooster. **"Give me more, give me more!** We will dance, we will entertain you and you will love us. We are the winners."

We were rock stars. Well, like old rock stars, but have you seen Mick lately? It was truly the high point of our competitive dance career. **Adrenaline flowing,** it was the high to end all highs. It felt overwhelming! I was alive and I was dancing with *my* star!

And, yes, we won that competition by a big margin. All those hours of practice paid off. Sue and Lester Smith were the new national champions. It sends shivers down my spine even to this day. It was the best—an ice-cream sundae with hot fudge, nuts and the cherry on the top, and boy, was all the work worth it. The following year, we defended our title and won it again. We had achieved our goal. After more than eight years of hard work and fun, we made it to the top of our dance Mt. Everest.

When you look at dancers on stage or on television, their grace and beauty belie the hours and hours of **nonstop athleticism required** to become proficient. No workout compares to the rigors of competitive dancing. It is hard work and hard on your body too.

Once I was sidelined while dancing the mambo and ended up having back surgery to repair a ruptured disk. By 2003 my hips had gyrated so much that I simply

272

Do you know what it takes to be a national ballroom champion?
Practice, practice and more practice, with a good dose of screaming by our coach Shirley Ballas!

wore one out. We finally hung up our dancing shoes when I had hip replacement surgery. For the record, I did get the "athletic" hip installed so I do have great range of motion and **I can exercise more.** Sue has had two injuries to her bicep tendon and rotator cuff which required major shoulder surgery. It was a dance related injury to her turning arm, likely due to too many turns over the years. Dancing really does take a toll on a senior body! Still, we would definitely do it all over again given the chance.

And here's the nugget I wish to share. We can do just about anything we set our minds on doing. All it takes for any of us is lots of dedication, lots of hard work, lots of dusting off and getting back on our feet to give it another try and practice, practice and more practice.

This works whether you want to dance, become a successful oilman, climb Mt. Everest or play the piano. This works no matter **what you seek to achieve in life.** Just make up your mind to be the very best that you can be. Why don't you give it a try? Why don't you **dance like no one's watching?** I promise you, no matter what you seek, you will become a champion, too. **Just for trying.**

274

Why don't you dance like no one's watching? I promise you, no matter what you seek, you will become a champion, too. **Just for trying.**

16

quality time remaining

Sue came down for breakfast one morning and delivered **a startling message** to me. "Lester, do you know what I was thinking about as I woke up this morning?"

"No, sweetie, what were you thinking?" She always comes up with the most interesting thoughts when she is in a super-relaxed state. That hazy area between sleep and wakefulness is one of **her most creative places.**

"Well, I don't think you're going to like what I have to say," she answered dryly.

OMG, what have I done wrong now? Guilt, guilt, guilt!

My mind ran through a mental rolodex of possibilities. Nothing, nada, zilch. I really hadn't had a chance to do anything out of line, as I had been home for the past two weeks recuperating from my most recent surgery. Of course, this didn't mean that something else from the more distant past might not bite me in the ass. You know what that's called? Jewish guilt.

I know, I know: "**What surgery now?** This old coot has already been under the knife loads of times. What parts were left to operate on?"

My latest bout had been a friendly reminder that cancer can creep up again at any time. This time, it left a calling card which read: esophageal cancer—near miss. That's a really big "C word." You catch that one late and you are toast, no butter, no jelly, just plain burnt toast.

In my case, it came without much warning except for a consistent burning chest pain. Could it possibly have been the six cups of coffee, the eight Red Bulls and the two energy shots that I was consuming on a daily basis that were causing me to have that awful acid reflux every night? I am **one pure, unadulterated adrenaline junkie**—I love the action, and I love the high that I get from massive doses of caffeine. I had been on quadruple doses of acid reflux medicine prescribed by my gastroenterologist for the past few years, and on a really bad night I would also gobble down as many as sixteen

Maalox tablets.

Anyway, to make a long story short—which is a big deal for me—I just plain ended up damaging my esophagus. They call it Barrett's Esophagus, and the cells had changed to high-grade dysplasia, which is one step and not many months away from cancer in situ, which any way you cut it becomes esophageal cancer. It has a 5 percent survival rate if caught real early. **Didn't like those odds at all.**

Here we go again, I thought. But this time it was three rounds of ablation therapy. This brand new ablation therapy uses high-frequency radio waves to literally burn away the damaged tissue. It worked on me, **thank goodness,** but I also required step two, which was laparoscopic surgery to repair my two major hernias. One was an incisional hernia, the result of the surgery that I had ten years ago, which removed my bladder and prostate. The muscle became loose right in the middle of my abs, right up close to my breast bone. Now, the second surgery to fix my hiatal hernia was a lot more complicated. It was called a Nissen Fundoplication, which is where they tighten and stitch up your loose diaphragm muscle and yank your esophagus, the part with the valve on the end, down below your diaphragm and wrap the top part of your stomach 360 degrees around it to hold it in place. I now have **enough Kevlar in my stomach to resurface Interstate 10** from Houston to Austin.

I was telling Melissa, my office manager of twenty years, about the surgery. I mentioned that with the valve below the diaphragm, I would **no longer be able**

to burp. She asked, "But Lester, what happens to all of the air that is trapped in your stomach?"

I speedily replied, "Here, pull my finger."

Uncle Adolph and Daddy taught me that one when I was four or five years old.

The doctor fibbed to me a wee bit. He said there would only be five puncture wounds in my abs from the laparoscopic surgery. It ended up being eleven. He said it was **the most he had ever done** on anyone. Oh great, I held a new record. Why couldn't it have been another gold medal for dancing? This was the most painful surgery I had ever been through. Pain meds do not work to relieve the pain from all of that inert gas that they pump in your tummy to do the surgery. My stomach looked as if I had swallowed **a forty-pound watermelon.** I was in the hospital for two days; then I had another two weeks of very intense pain. I was scared this time, real scared, and so was Sue. I had her call the rabbi to come over to our home and pray for me. I thought I was going to die. But two weeks later I started getting back to my old self and the doctors said I would be back in the gym in six weeks. The watermelon even went away and left me with a nice flat, skinny tummy.

But back to where I started, right about the time I started feeling a little better. So Sue said I wasn't going to like what she had to say. Well, here's what it was: "Honey, it's inevitable that we are going to grow old and die, and there is absolutely nothing that we can do about it. **It happens to everyone**; nobody gets out of this

280

deal alive."

She continued, "So we need to enjoy each phase of our life, including the older part, and look forward to **what happens next**—when we die. The only thing we can do is take really good care of ourselves since we'll probably **live to be over a hundred."** Pretty sharp cookie. Once again, she had hit the nail directly on the head.

Oh my, Sue is so smart and so beautiful, so elegant, and **we are so hard in love** with each other. We have been together for more than twenty years and we still act like a couple of newlyweds. I wonder if that testosterone the doctor put me on years ago has anything to do with that? You bet your sweet ass it does. I'm nearly seventy, think I'm forty and act like I'm nineteen. All that exercise means I'm fit and I'm ripped and loving every minute of it. The reason Sue stays so thin is that I'm chasing her around the house all the time. And she lets me win a bunch, a whole bunch. And that's why we always have those **perpetual grins** on our faces.

I slept on Sue's inspired thoughts. Interesting, very interesting. I got up the next morning, **thank goodness**, went into the bathroom and looked at my face in the mirror. There it was, as plain as day, right on my forehead—one of those darn **grocery store bar codes** that have an expiration date on them. Soap sure wouldn't scrub it off; maybe a little Botox would hide it from everyone, but it was still going to be there. We're all born with it. Look closely. If you're over fifty years old you can start to see yours too. It's commonly known as "wrinkles." Darn things just won't go away. I guess

This is what's all about—laughing, loving and giving with all your heart.

I could have a brow lift and pull the skin up tight and make it go away. Like that would really work for a bald guy: "Hey look at that silly bald guy with that big scar on top of his head. If you look real close you can see his bar code." **Damn, I hate getting old.**

But **what was I going to do?** Sue was right as rain, spot on. We are going to get old and die. As they used to say on "Dragnet," just the facts, ma'am, just the facts. It was plain as the bar code on my face. Those were the facts. What's a guy to do? Well, I got this one figured out in a big hurry—and actually I realized I had been living like this for years.

It was just like the first step of AA. We admitted that we have an expiration date and that we are going to die one day. Step two, we came to believe that a power greater than ourselves could **restore us to sanity.** And step three, we made a decision to turn our lives and will over to the care of God as we understood Him. Those steps worked great for me, and I have been a card-carrying member of AA for more than thirty-five years. I'm coming up on ten years sober. It works for dealing with addiction, so why wouldn't it work for dealing with that blasted expiration date on your forehead? Well, guess what? It does.

Was I going to approach my expiration date like a carton of milk, getting more and more sour as the years ticked past? That is definitely not my style. Why not grow old like a bottle of rare, red Burgundy, getting better and better the older I get? And here's the

283

big secret: **it's an inside job**, not an outside job. We get to choose how we feel and think about aging. All of us have the key that fits the lock inside our heads. If we keep fiddling with that key until we find the lock, we'll hear it go "CLICK."

Here's how.

First of all, **get off your butt**. Turn off the television and computer, put down your Crackberry and make an appointment with your doctor to make sure your ticker can handle some exercise. Start slowly with a daily thirty-minute walk. Get a dog—or two or three—and take them for daily walks. And if you don't have a dog, go to the SPCA or Humane Society and **walk their dogs**. Take your sweetie to Memorial Park or just out walking in the neighborhood. Hold hands and listen…there is a whole lot of nature to observe. Enjoy the fresh air and all that comes with it. Ramp it up a bit and join the Avon Walk or Susan G. Komens Race for the Cure. Really ramp it up and head to the YMCA or your favorite gym. I'm inspired by some of the people I see working out on a regular basis. My **idol at the gym** is Irvin Gordon. He's eighty-five, and he works out for hours every day. **All the young chicks flirt with him**. I think he flirts back a lot too. Now that is my idea of a great bottle of perfectly balanced red wine. And that is exactly how I want it to be.

Lay off the smokes, drink in moderation and use good judgment in what you put into your body. Thinking more "green" than white or red is a great way to change your look as well as your outlook. Get enough rest, breathe deeply and remember that

laughter really is the best medicine.

If you're not already approaching your expiration date like this, why don't you give my way a try for the next ninety days? I promise you—and you can take this to the bank —you'll feel better, look better and you'll be well on your way to finding that keyhole in your brain. When you do, **you'll hear the big "click."**

So, do you want to be a carton of milk or do you want to be a very rare bottle of Chateau Lafite? **Do you want to live each day like it could be your last?** Do you want to embrace it, flirt with it and revel in it? Well, you can. Remember, it's an inside job and the choice is all yours. Try those first three steps from AA—whether you've ever had a drink or not. I promise you, they work. Just do it, and be all that you can be. We've all heard that before, but it's really possible. And remember—you will always enjoy that beautiful cabernet or Burgundy more when you can share it with someone special. **Cheers to your new life!** Drink it up!

17

finding life in the obituaries

Ever read the obituaries? For a long time I couldn't read them. Perhaps I was simply afraid to find my own name there among the many smiling faces staring back at me.

I would always tell the story to anyone who would listen that if I woke up in the morning and didn't see my name in the obituaries, then I knew **I was going to have a pretty good day.**

Of course that was one of my pirated sayings, but with all of my heart I knew my time on earth was about to expire. When you have cancer, **you think about dying** pretty much all the time. It becomes a sort of creepy game.

If you have never had cancer or a serious illness, you can't fully grasp the **magnitude of this statement.** You may think you understand, but as I keep telling you: "You don't get it till you've got it." And I've got it. Been there, done that. In fact, I've been there way too many times. The thought of dying is with me constantly, just about as often as I take a breath. Regardless of what I do, what mind games I play, what activities I do, the thought of death will just not go away. It's with me every waking moment; it is the last thing I think about before I go to sleep; **it's what I dream about,** what I think about when I get up in the middle of the night over and over again, and it's the very first thing I think about when I wake up in the morning. No amount of whiskey can make that bogey man go away either. Believe me, I would know. When you are fighting cancer, that mean bastard just won't leave you alone, no matter how much you beg or plead.

And you can't quite shake it because it rears its ugly head every time some well-meaning person asks, "How are you doing?" or states, "I know exactly how you feel," or "Don't worry, you're going to be okay."

Really? Promise?

Or, I love this one: a well-meaning friend would take Sue aside and whisper, "How

"He's only got minutes left, poor dear, so we should be going. Wouldn't want him **to drop dead right** here and now, would we?"

obituary:

A notice of the death of a person, often with a biographical sketch, as in a newspaper

is Lester *really* doing? Is he really going to be okay?" I told her to tell them, "He's only got minutes left, poor dear, so we should be going. Wouldn't want him to drop dead right here and now, would we?"

Seriously, I would nod, smile and say "Thank you, thank you for asking, I feel fine." But under my breath, with gritted teeth, I would say, "Bullshit, **you don't have the slightest idea how I feel,** and I am relatively confident you don't know whether I am going to live or die." Or, "If you ask me that question one more time, I'm going to knock your lights out."

I have been cancer-free for more than nine years. People still ask the same questions, and we still give the same answers. They all mean well, but I sure wish they would ask me about the weather instead. I'd rather not have cancer as **the focus of my life,** but unfortunately, it does rather make headline news in your own reality show. And, every time it comes up, I think about writing my own obituary again.

So I decided that maybe I really did need to write it. And one day, I sat down with pen and paper and started to write. Talk about depressing. I mean, I had been really successful in the oil business, but what else had I done? As I stared at *The New York Times* one morning reading about these men and women who had gone on to "be with their Lord and Savior," or "entered into the eternal presence of angels," I wondered what would be said about me. I wasn't at all sure I believed in angels; in fact, **I wasn't sure that my one way ticket was marked "north."** South seemed a whole lot more likely.

Lester H. Smith: He was a really successful oilman.

Or . . . Lester H. Smith: He was a really successful bald oilman.

Or . . . Lester H. Smith: He really caught some big fish.

In an effort to get inspired, I began to religiously read *The New York Times* and *Houston Chronicle* obituary section every day. Fascinating reading, really. I took note of the really young people who had died. The hardest of all was seeing a baby's or a child's obituary. That really seemed unfair. I guess all of us can reason that an eighty- or ninety-year-old somehow has had a great life, so it doesn't seem so sad.

But in fact, it is always sad. Someone really loved that sweet old man. He was someone's father or grandfather, and some decades earlier, someone's baby. He was a veteran, he was a truck driver, he was a Boy Scout leader. Someone thought about him every single day, worried about him and in the end, visited him in the hospital. I hope someone was with him, holding his hand, when he died. **Someone aches for him right now**—maybe many people, hundreds, who knows? How many lives did this gentleman touch? What would people say about him now that he was gone? "God, I miss him so much. I just wish he could have lived a little longer."

These thoughts lingered each time I read the daily paper and wondered, what my own obituary would look like.

A little while ago, September 13, 2008, to be exact, I received an envelope from one of my brothers. Inside was a note:

"Lester, I know you would want to have a copy of this. Daddy has been dead for exactly forty eight years."

It was the obituary written and read by Rabbi Rosenberg at our father's funeral a few days after his death on September 13, 1960.

With shaking hands I began to read that precious obituary written four decades earlier. My eyes blurred with tears as I read of my dad's love of his family, his community and his faith in God. How he was a friend to everyone and a stranger to none. How his family came to Wharton from Eastern Europe to find their Shangri-la in the clay fields of this East Texas community and became one of our town's pillars.

The man on paper was indeed my father, but he was so much more to me than anyone could fathom. Did anyone know how he cared for me when he thought I had food poisoning and I threw up all over him at two in the morning? Well, truth be told, it wasn't food poisoning, it was too much Mogen David at a Bar Mitzvah. **I think Daddy knew it, too.**

Did anyone know that at five foot-ten inches tall, he was a **giant to me?** Did anyone know how safe I felt in his arms the night the hurricane came? Did anyone know that on my seventh birthday, I told him I wanted to be an oilman, just like him? Did anyone know how much I loved him and missed him?

My brother and I were attending the University of Oklahoma, the same college our

My father, Maynard Smith, had the best smile.

father had attended, when we got the call that he was really sick and we needed to come home right away. **We took the first plane** back to Houston, praying all the way that he was going to be okay. The long faces at the airport gate told us that our prayers had not been answered. That hour-long drive from Houston to Wharton took an eternity, and we both cried uncontrollably all the way back home. He was only forty-six when he died of a massive heart attack.

I remember the total shock of it all—how could this be? He had done so many wonderful things for so many people, he was so loved and respected, he was the man I patterned my life after, the man I loved and respected above all others. He was going to be my oil partner, I was growing up to be just like him. And now what? I felt so lost and alone. How could I ever think of moving forward with my life? The immense burden of grief felt suffocating.

I put on a suit and sat with my mourning family on the first row in the synagogue. I remember how cold I felt, how packed the synagogue was and the quiet of the house. I don't remember hearing the rabbi's words; perhaps I was simply too grief-stricken to hear anything but the buzz in my own head.

These precious words on the paper I held brought it all back to me. **I sobbed with my head in my hands,** and I knew it was time to finally close the emotional door on much of that boyhood grief. When I read his obituary, I knew then what mine would look like. I was, and am, just like my father. I am flesh of his flesh; he taught me well, and I know with no uncertainty that he would be proud of the man I have become. I finally felt at peace with myself.

The Wharton Synagogue closed in 1998, but before the final service, I visited the temple and the Maynard Smith Memorial Library that we dedicated to my father's memory. **My dad was a voracious reader,** digesting *The New York Times, Houston Post* and *Houston Chronicle* in a coffee-drinking morning ritual. He would have loved the library we built to honor him.

These monuments to those who have gone before us lend us a deep and insightful look into our own lives. As I walked among the volumes in my dad's library, I couldn't help but wonder which words he would use to describe his own life. What words do we use to describe our own?

It's often in the passing of a loved one that **we learn to embrace life.** Or faced with the notion of our own demise, we begin to see our lives in a new slant. We crave opportunities to celebrate life and its vibrancy, perhaps as a way to offset and even defeat the inevitable. Death will come knocking. We just don't want to be at home when the doorbell rings. And we certainly don't want to be home alone.

Because **we believe in the strength of numbers.** We believe that united we stand strong, and a strong front wins. The bogey man won't come into a room when Daddy is there; isn't that what every child believes?

This bogey man called cancer is one bad dude, and yes, I may

Daddy, my brother Stephen and I
at the park in Wharton in 1945.

succumb to its grip someday. But not today. I can't worry about it anymore. I cannot, and will not, let it define who I am. I choose to live my life through the warmth and love of my family, friends and a community that has embraced and supported me.

Looking death in the eye over and over again during my seventeen-year battle with cancer has taught me how **very fragile and precious life is,** and for that I am grateful. Anyone who knows me also knows I am no angel, and my one-way ticket may indeed take me to a warmer climate. But as I have contemplated death, I have also learned to love more deeply, dance much longer and embrace each day surrounded by my dear ones.

Perhaps as I have contemplated my own obituary, I have learned a thing or two about life. And perhaps in the end I have indeed found the perfect words to end it all: **Lester H. Smith, one bald, life-loving oilman.**

Baby Lester at eighteen months. Where did all that hair go?

298

And that may be the perfect ending to a life not just well lived, but more importantly, a life well loved.

18

little drops of water make a river

It was opening night, and I was a nervous wreck. My blue and white striped satin jockey suit was uncomfortable, and I was worried that I might slip on the polished wood stage during my dance routine. As our dance coach lined us up just behind the curtain stage left, I looked over at my friend Jimmy, whose baby blue satin pants were taking on a darker hue—right at the crotch. Well, at least **I wasn't that nervous.** I went on stage solo and tap danced to Camptown Races. When I finished, everyone in the Jewish Community Center stood and applauded wildly. At age four, **Lester the Entertainer was born!**

YOU GOTTA DANCE LIKE NO ONE'S WATCHING

When I think back on the wonderful childhood that I had in Wharton I have to give credit to two organizations that truly molded me and deeply impacted my life—Hadassah and the Boy Scouts.

Hadassah is a volunteer women's organization **dedicated to strengthening and enriching the Jewish community** here in America, while supporting many efforts in Israel, especially education and healthcare. There is no doubt that the organization and its presence in Wharton helped make the little boy dancing to "Camptown Races," become **the man that he is today.**

As an active member and president of the Wharton Hadassah chapter, my mother worked tirelessly with many others in the community to further the ideals of the organization's founder, Henrietta Szold. Growing up Jewish in a small Texas town was a kind of Norman Rockwell experience for me. Picture the image of the family gathered around a table, forks ready to devour a beautiful turkey hot out of the oven. Only instead of turkey, we had a brisket. Come to think of it, it seemed the entire **Jewish community centered around the kitchen**—or in my case—the kitchen table. My Jewish upbringing and life in Wharton were inextricably linked to my stomach.

Every holiday and event—from a bris to a Bar Mitzvah, from Passover to Purim— was marked by **traditional Jewish foods.** Rosh Hashanah, or the Jewish new year, was marked by sweets. At Passover my brothers, cousins and I always had fun finding the *Afikomen*—a piece of matzo that was hidden before the seder began. There was

My first time on stage dancing to "Camptown Races." Lester the Entertainer was born!

*I have so many fond memories of growing up
in Wharton with a house filled with laughter and joy.*

*Maurice and Esther Jessell, my maternal grandparents,
otherwise known as Grandpa and Ettie. I remember
Ettie in the kitchen, always baking up something
warm, sweet and doughy. Maybe that's where
my doughnut passion was born!*

always a nice brisket after we got through the bitter herbs and boiled egg.

Hanukkah meant latkes, potato pancakes, and my favorite food of all time—*doughnuts*. My *bubbe* also made Jewish penicillin, a.k.a. matzo ball soup. Her matzo balls were perfect—not too soft, not too hard. We called her matzo balls "floaters"—as opposed to "sinkers." And no matter what ailed me, I always felt better after a huge bowlful. Years later, when I was home from the hospital after my cancer surgery, matzo ball soup was the ticket to recovery.

We love food so much in my family that my daughter even collected family recipes and **created a wonderful cookbook.** Who knew there were nine different brisket recipes? For the record, I love them *all*.

You know what I love most about the meals? Sitting down together at the table and listening to each other's stories. I am sure that my knack for storytelling is a direct result of sitting with my parents and my brothers and often, extended family members and friends. **Food builds a community,** and for me, that was central to Jewish life in Wharton.

The Hadassah ladies (as I called them) were always holding fund-raising events around food. There were bake sales, lunches and dinners nearly every month and an annual barbecue in June. I think half the town showed up for that wonderful event. They held clothing drives too. I remember my cousin Freddie packing up clothes to send to Israel, while I worked at a charity rummage sale, providing clothes to the area's migrant

My beautiful mother, Rosalie, with my brother Stephen and me in 1944.

workers. There is no doubt that **Wharton produced some characters** (that would be me) and one of the world's most respected civic leaders—my cousin Fred Zeidman. He was appointed Chairman of the United States Holocaust Memorial Council by President George W. Bush in 2002 and is just about the finest man I know.

My work ethic was definitely influenced by **watching my mother** and her friends in their effort to make the world—and I do mean the world—a better place. That vision extended way beyond our little Texas town to link our very American way of life with our Jewish heritage and our roots in Israel. My mother's active participation in Hadassah was one of the greatest influences in my life. It taught me, in the words of the late Hadassah founder Henrietta Szold, to **"dream . . . and dream big."** Now me, "dream big" is my middle name, even to this day. I just don't know how to operate any other way.

When I wasn't selling cakes at the Hadassah bake sale, I was hawking snow cones and candy for the Boy Scouts. Scouting was a natural outcome of growing up in a small Texas oil town. Of course, the lure of Boy Scouts for me was all the great camping trips, building fires with flint, constructing a lean-to and perfecting the art of making s'mores.

You know, **s'more making is a lost art.** You have to make sure the marshmallow is toasted just enough to melt the chocolate but not hot enough to burn your tongue. It takes loads of practice but what the heck—it's an art form! I can make killer s'mores. And I learned this from an incredible cook—my mother, the Hadassah-president-turned-cub-scout-den-mother.

Of course scouting is so much more than fires and camping. It taught me values like **trust, responsibility, self-reliance, teamwork and what it means to be a good citizen.** The fun part was I got to learn all of this while being outdoors, doing community service and sometimes sleeping under the East Texas stars. I just loved being a Boy Scout. I liked it so much that I remained active in Boy Scouts until I was in high school. I can still recite the Scout Oath:

On my honor, I will do my best

To do my duty to God and my country;

To obey the Scout Law;

To help other people at all times;

To keep myself physically strong, mentally awake and morally straight.

Well, outside of morally straight, **I have done pretty well.** I might have made Eagle Scout if there was a badge for inappropriate behavior or partying, or let's just say, behavior unbecoming to a Scout.

Regardless of how much I may have strayed from the straight and narrow path that was the backbone of my upbringing, I guess the most important lesson I learned from my parents and scouting was this: **we have a moral obligation to be generous.**

Dear Mr. Lester Smith,

We deeply appreciate your donation to our troop, we are going to be using the money for scolarships for Scouts that can't pay to go on trips like the one we are about to take to Philmont. Philmont is a trip our eagle scouts are planning to take in a few months. We will also be using the money for our summer camp we have every year for our kids in our troop that can't come up with the money to go. Again we deeply appreciate your donation.

Sincerely
Troop 232 Scribe, Morgan Zoland

Boys Scouts and Jewish life was all I knew in Wharton.
Even after 59 years, I still remain active in Scouting. 1953.

And generosity can take many forms. It comes in the way of **what God has given us.** And no matter what that gift is—go out and share it.

As I write these words, I know that the first thing you will think is this: "Lester's talking about money." But that's only part of it.

I have witnessed acts of selflessness and compassion that have moved me to tears. I have seen **simple acts of kindness and respect for others change lives.** I have seen the power of generosity in all its forms, over and over again—and you can be just as generous, no matter the size of your wallet.

Be generous in your spirit, in sharing your passion for life, generous in your time and if you can, be generous with your checkbook too. Big or small, it doesn't really matter. Little drops of water make a river. It's just about giving it all away.

Be generous in your spirit, in sharing your passion for life, generous in your time and if you can, be generous with your checkbook too. **Big or small,** it doesn't really matter. Little drops of water make a river. It's just about giving it all away.

It's all over folks—and they lived happily ever after. The End.